METHODISM

Her Unfinished Task

By

W. E. SANGSTER

METHODIST PREACHER

LONDON: THE EPWORTH PRESS

Published by

THE EPWORTH PRESS

(FRANK H. CUMBERS)

25–35 City Road, London, E.C.1

*

New York   .   Toronto

Melbourne   .   Capetown

TO
'THE PEOPLE CALLED METHODISTS'

With
Much Affection
and
Warm Gratitude
but
In Deepening Concern

MADE AND PRINTED IN GREAT BRITAIN

METHODISM

Her Unfinished Task

PREFACE

THIS BOOK is intended for the people to whom it is dedicated. On a previous occasion—at the Bicentenary of John Wesley's conversion—I was bold enough to address them in a book entitled *Methodism Can Be Born Again*, the message of which I have seen no reason to modify or retract.

But the passing years have not lessened my concern. A fear gnaws at my heart that this people may miss the opportunities of the hour and fail in the work to which God has called them. No Church can do her work effectively if she grows unsure of what that work is.

The Churches are drawing closer together. The Ecumenical Movement grows in appeal and power. The conviction that Christians belong to one another as well as to their Lord has led them to overleap barriers of race and class and denomination and to rejoice that the things which unite them are infinitely more important than the things which divide.

But denominations are not destroyed. No Communion comes into being, persists through the centuries, and begets its company of saints except by the will and the blessing of God, and the Ecumenical Movement does not foresee at the last a vast Communion every part of which is just a replica of every other part, but a family large and loving enough to enjoy the differences which God Himself has blessed.

One cannot belong *now* to a Church which 'is yet to be' except as one recognizes that *whatever will be, is*, and that the future lies in the womb of the present. One cannot belong to the Church which is everywhere—unless we belong to it somewhere. Sharp criticism of denominationalism in all its forms is, therefore, often unreflecting. A man can love his corps and love the army too. A man can love his denomination and love the Holy Catholic Church. So far from these two loves being antithetical, they are part of the same great affection.

Let a man be on his guard against overstressing his denominational peculiarities in such a way that he is unbalanced in his witness to the Christian Faith as a whole, and only good can come of his careful tending and sharing of those precious parts of truth which God gave him and his friends so plainly to see.

I belong to the Holy Catholic Church in Methodism. There God saved my soul and set me to work. I do not think my fellow-Methodists overstress their denominational peculiarities. Indeed, in their serious pursuit of organic Church union their tendency is often to disparage their own individuality and live half unconscious of their special contribution to the Church as a whole.

I hope this book may serve to remind them of this. If the stress falls upon denominational peculiarities, that is not because they are more important than the things shared with others but only that we may believe that even these peculiarities are dear to God. Some of them, it is true, are important only for the years that must intervene before a closer union is consummated, but others partake of permanence because they contribute to the Church which no man sees as yet (except with the eye of faith) but which we believe, by the power of God, is yet to be.

There is a work still for Methodism to do. It matters to the whole body of Christians. It matters now and it will matter in eternity. Its true discharge will bring nearer that glorious day when all the ransomed Church of God is saved, to sin no more.

Controversial things are said here, but nothing is set down in uncharitableness. If, unwittingly, these words wound anyone, I sincerely ask their pardon. If I am mistaken in the opinions I express (and I am sharply aware that I may be), I am mistaken after much prayer.

I am deeply indebted to the Rev. Dr. Charles Ryder Smith for reading the typescript and making many helpful suggestions, and to my friend and secretary, Mr. P. E. Found, for lightening the labour in every way that he could.

W. E. SANGSTER

The Central Hall
  Westminster
    S.W.1

CONTENTS

CHAPTER ONE

THERE *IS* AN UNFINISHED TASK

I⊤ sometimes happens, in the history of human thought and effort, that a powerful movement or institution, which has mightily served its generation, dies, and dies with the willing consent of those who inspired it. It is not death by decay but death by fulfilment. The movement has done its work and achieved its end. A change of custom, an Act of Parliament, the destruction of something evil against which the movement had pitted its strength, has been gloriously completed, and the movement can now as gloriously die.

No death could be finer. The Greeks had a special word to describe it. They called it 'euthanasia', a word which has changed its meaning with passing time but which originally meant 'well-dying'—the noble end of something finished, completed, rounded-off.

Some years ago, in the city of Hull, I went into the house of William Wilberforce. It is a museum now of the Anti-Slavery Agitation. Hanging on the wall there were bills of sale of 'prime slaves'; there were pictures of the torture black men endured in captivity; there were details innumerable of the great organization which William Wilberforce led. It was interesting—but it was a *museum*. The battle had been won—more than one hundred years before. There are slaves still in the world but they are not in the British Empire. The Anti-Slavery Movement splendidly fulfilled itself and came splendidly to its euthanasia.

Is Methodism nearing its euthanasia? Will the historian of the future, commenting on the movement, say something like this:

It lasted a little more than two hundred years. A mighty influence in the eighteenth century, it was still powerful in the nineteenth, but when the twentieth century began it was already a waning force. So far as England was concerned, it had lost its *raison d'être*. The cold formalism of the Church of England, against which the early Methodists protested with such vehemence, had largely gone: the Established Church had found its soul. The evil social conditions which excited the condemnation of Wesley's followers had been changed almost beyond belief. Indeed, the State had taken over much of the remedial service previously rendered by these and other Christians and called it 'progress'. Fulfilling its mission, the movement died. . . .?

Will it be like that? Has the time come for the obsequies? Or has God a use for Methodism still?

Most thoughtful Methodists would agree that Methodism matters no more than it matters to God, but how much does it matter to Him? Have we still a divine mission to fulfil in the world? Is it true that if our candle were extinguished one bright light would go out in the candelabra of Heaven? How much does Methodism matter to God?

The people who believe that God has only the slightest use for Methodism beg us to observe what has happened in France and Canada, and in South India too. They remind us that Methodism has disappeared as a denomination in France. The little French Methodist Church has been merged into the Protestant Church of that country. Methodism has disappeared as a distinctive communion in Canada, and many of its friends feel that it has largely lost its warmth with its identity. It has disappeared as a separate denomination in South India as well.

'These are the signs of the times,' some observers say, 'and they point plainly to this: that we ought to work for reunion as swiftly and as advantageously as we can, being glad if our witness can still be impressive in the larger whole which will then be achieved.' A couple of generations ago our fathers had a vision of Methodism engirdling the globe and becoming, herself, a world power for righteousness, but that vision has largely faded in the light of modern day.

The question whether or not Methodism has fulfilled its task in the world cannot possibly be answered without first asking: What *was* Methodism's task in the world? For what purpose did God raise this people up?

No answer need be given to the people who say that it never had a task and that *God* never raised it up: that it was merely another illustration (in Burke's phrase) of 'the dissidence of Dissent'.[1] That can be left to the judgement of history. There is no lack of historians who, with no particular bias in favour of Wesley's followers, have been eager to testify to the purging and healing influences this movement has exerted upon the world.[2] Indeed, there is some evidence for believing that it is the greatest tide of the Spirit since Pentecost.[3]

Divine in origin, what was the divine *purpose* at its heart? Called into being by God, what work did God design that it should do?

1. John Wesley always insisted that the purpose of Methodism was to 'spread scriptural holiness throughout the land'. The phrase sounds a little archaic today but no man can miss the meaning. The people were to be made

[1] *Speech on Moving Resolutions for Conciliation with the Colonies, 22nd March 1775.*
[2] Lecky, *History of England in the Eighteenth Century*, Vol. III, pp. 48ff. (edit. 1901). Halévy, *A History of the English People in 1815*, Vol. I, pp. 372, 389f., 393, 399f.
[3] Bett, *The Spirit of Methodism*, p. 10.

Christ-like. Has it been done? In an age when our hoardings seem all to carry necessary warnings about venereal disease; when divorce statistics out-soar all previous records; when petty pilfering is widespread and there are no towels on our trains because they were stolen at the rate of 28,000 *a week*;[1] and when juvenile delinquency was never more serious—can it be said that scriptural holiness is spread throughout the land? Can it be argued that the work is finished? Would those other agencies working to the same end willingly lose this ally? Would the whole Body of God consent to the amputation of so stout a limb?

2. But the making of people Christ-like always pre-supposes an earlier task: evangelism. The influence of Christ on any man or woman is limited and indirect until that man or woman willingly surrenders his or her will to the Divine Master. Conversion (howsoever described) is a pre-condition of superlative goodness. That was why Wesley and his early helpers bent their whole strength to reaching plain people with the offer of Christ.

They set no theoretical limit to their sphere of operations. Wesley said: 'The world is my parish.' He scorned parochialism. When Bishop Butler reproved him for preaching in Bristol and said: 'You have no business here: you are not commissioned to preach in this diocese. Therefore I advise you to go hence', Wesley replied: 'My lord, my business on earth is to do what good I can. Wherever, therefore, I think I can do most good there must I stay, so long as I think so. At present I think I can do most good here; therefore, here I stay.'[2]

If he left Wales largely to Howell Harris (because, of course, he couldn't speak Welsh),[3] he took Ireland and

---

[1] *Hansard*, Vol. 382, col. 1228.
[2] *Journal*, Vol. II, pp. 256f. (footnote) (16th August 1739).
[3] ibid., Vol. III, p. 311.

Scotland into his itinerary with all England, and sent his gallant lieutenants to America as well.

His followers never forgot his vision of a world-parish. If one includes the missionary activity not only of British Methodism but of the daughter Methodist Churches in the United States, in Australasia, and in South Africa as well, it is astonishingly true that there is hardly a country of any size in this wide world where Methodist missionaries are not active. No one who has not taken the trouble to examine this work in detail would credit its extent. If adherents are added to full-members, the world community of Methodism is estimated now at fifty million souls.

But who could say that the world-parish is evangelized? In round figures there are 420 million in China: less than four million are Christian. There are 353 million in India: about six million are Christian.

Methodism, apart from her responsibilities at home, shares the task of world evangelism with all other branches of the Christian Church, but in many wide and needy areas hers is the only witness to Christian truth.

But the chief evangelical responsibility of British Methodism is, of course, in Britain itself. The advance abroad cannot blind us to the retreat at home. The net loss of full-members in British Methodism in the last twelve years was 75,064, an awful figure which no amount of dubious 'explanation' can explain away. We may be grateful that these are signs that the tide has turned.

Nor would it matter much to the whole Church of God if this decline were confined to Methodism. Alas! it would appear from the 'returns' of those Communions which publish clear figures (not a common ecclesiastical virtue!) that all sections of the organized Church in our land are falling back and making little impression on the wide areas of paganism. Indeed, the Church of England seems to think that the time has come to do Augustine's work over again and called its moving report on the religious situation *Towards the Conversion of England*. Any branch of the Church which knows the way to the people's heart, or can employ an evangelical method to reach the need of some classes of the people, is under special responsibility to exert her whole strength in this age.

Methodism has shown a ready adaptability to evangelical needs. Admitting, as one must, that the drift from the Churches has not been arrested, it is freely allowed in her sister Communions that by her great Central Halls and Missions, and by her Commando Campaigns (to mention only two characteristic activities), this Church has not forgotten the commission of her founder and carries the cause of evangelism warm in her heart.

But is the task finished? Should we not rather say that it has barely begun?

3. It was a great mercy of God to England (and indirectly to the world) that when the problems created by the Industrial Revolution first began to be oppressive, a great tide of spiritual life was running through the land.

Evil things were not allowed to arise utterly unchallenged. If the leaders of the Evangelical Revival had no complete answer to the most awkward social questions of the hour—and they had not—they could at least recognize them as ugly problems and indict each evil as a sin. The religious awakening of the eighteenth century has long been regarded as a watershed from which many healing streams have flowed into our communal life. Methodism was never allowed to degenerate into pietism. It kept close to life.

Wesley deferred his dying to send a letter of warm encouragement to Wilberforce in his battle against slavery,[1] and John Howard, the prison reformer, shared

[1] *Letters*, Vol. VIII, p. 265 (24th February 1791).

that apostolic enheartenment too. Lord Shaftesbury was glad to trace his inspiration to the same spiritual source.[1] It is not surprising that five of the six Tolpuddle Martyrs (who were among the first to suffer in the long battle for a living wage) were Methodists, nor that so many of the most prominent of the early labour leaders found their spiritual nourishment among this people.

Yet who would say today that the relation of religion to social progress is clearly understood both inside and outside the Church? There are still devout people within the Church who plead that religion and politics must be kept apart (as though they ever could!), and not a few folk outside the Church, passionate for social improvement, who declare that religion is their implacable foe and 'the opium of the people'.[2]

Can it be argued, then, that Methodism's social ministry is at an end? In an age when most men are crying out for a new economic order, is not the need for this reconciling word greater than ever? Indeed, is not the need rather a great *expansion* of Methodism's historic mission, carrying the service beyond social salvage work to a deep spiritual sociology and economics . . . and is not the task as urgent as it is vital?

These, then, were the main tasks for which the Methodists were raised up. To spread holiness throughout the land. To evangelize. To Christianize the social order.

It is not suggested for a moment that no other branch of the Church of Christ had any concern over these things —even in the eighteenth century. I repeat that when one

[1] J. Wesley Bready, *Lord Shaftesbury and Social-Industrial Progress*, p. 389.
[2] This phrase is sometimes ascribed in its origin to Charles Kingsley (Alexander Miller, *The Christian Significance of Karl Marx*, p. 40. See also *Encyclopaedia Britannica*, 14th edn., Vol. V, p. 639). But I can find it no earlier in Kingsley's works than 27th May 1848 (*Politics for the People*, p. 58), where he speaks of the Bible as 'an opium-dose'. Karl Marx used it in the *Deutsch-Französische Jahrbücher*, February 1844.

speaks of the 'distinctive' mission of a Communion, one does not, and cannot, imply that that mission is *exclusively* held by that group of Christians but only that it is characteristic of them and a chief concern. No one intimate with the life of England in the eighteenth century would deny that degree of distinctiveness to the Methodists, and no one intimate with this Communion today would dissent from the view that when she is most herself the stress still falls with a certain inevitability on these three tasks: Holiness, Evangelism, The Social Gospel.

But the years have brought their other tasks as well.

4. In the passing of two centuries Methodism has become a '*bridge-Church*'. A prophet might have foreseen it. John Wesley himself was the product of generations of Church and Dissent.[1] His parents were rigidly Anglican but both his maternal grandfather and his paternal great-grandfather were ejected from their livings by the Act of Uniformity. All his four grandparents were dissenters.

Both strains were in the founder of Methodism— and both strains are in his followers too. The militant kind of Nonconformist, to whom the Anglican Church is a near relative of 'the Scarlet Woman', has always found a typical Methodist tepid. He has charged him on occasion (especially if he was of the Wesleyan section of reunited British Methodism) with being 'churchy'; of taking the Holy Communion the Anglican way; of making his Book of Offices on the Prayer Book model; of displaying no zeal in the movement for disestablishment. There is pith in all the charges. Methodists have had to suffer with their fellow-Free Churchmen the

[1] Arnold Lunn, *John Wesley*, p. 22. R. F. Wearmouth, *Methodism and the Common People of the Eighteenth Century*, p. 11. *Dictionary of National Biography*, Vol. 34, p. 73.

discourtesies and condescensions which the less estimable kind of clergyman sometimes displays,[1] but the denomination as a denomination could never burn with separatist zeal. Perhaps that is because the Anglicans never hanged the pioneers of Methodism as they hanged the brave pioneers of other Free Churches: Penry and Greenwood and Barrowe, grandly maintaining that 'Christ is the only head of His Church and His laws may no man alter'.[2]

But, whatever the reason, the fact is there. It is rooted in history. The Methodist was never separatist on principle. He held the same faith as his Anglican friend, but—as Matthew Arnold is reported to have said—it was 'religion in earnest'. Thrust from the bosom of the Church in which he would fain have stayed, he could not and cannot forget the mother who suckled him, and if he has ranged himself now, not merely of necessity but of conviction, at the side of Free Churchmen, he does so with a knowledge and an affection for the Anglican Church which is unique in Nonconformity.

A ministry lies at the heart of that uniqueness.

Methodism is a bridge-Church between the Anglican and the other Free Churches. It links hands easily both ways. It belongs to one, but it can easily interpret the other. As the will of God in the reunion of His dismembered Church becomes clearer to all, and wins a worthy response, this ministry of reconciliation will become yet more important. It increases in importance year by year. It is just one bridge in a series of bridges, and does not span the deepest or widest gulf, but those most concerned to find the road of reunion are sure that this is a necessary part of the royal way.

[1] Bishop Hensley Henson warned his clergy against 'the hurtful and supercilious exclusiveness, as absurd as it is offensive, which has too often marked the attitude of Anglicans toward Nonconformists' (*Bishoprick Papers*, p. 126).

[2] Ernest A. Payne, *The Free Church Tradition in the Life of England*, pp. 33f.

5. Nor is that the only new task which the passage of 200 years has brought to Methodism.

It has a special ministry in rural areas as well.

The Christian religion is offered to the people of this country in two chief ways: the sacerdotal and the evangelical. Some men argue that these are mutually exclusive: it is 'either or . . .'. Others believe that both are true interpretations of the Gospel and correspond to the priestly and prophetic functions in the ministry. 'Ultimately,' say these thinkers, 'both ways of interpreting the faith must be synthesized.'

But that is not yet. Whether or not they *can* be synthesized, and how, and when, belongs to the future. In the meanwhile, it is 'either or . . .', and that has consequences in rural England not always realized by people who live in towns. If the vicar of the village church is an Anglo-Catholic zealot, aiming to out-Roman the Romans, robbing the interior of his parish church of half its Englishness, and giving it that strangely foreign and Italianate appearance some of these earnest men prefer, not a few of the people in the parish are estranged. They are not estranged chiefly by appearances. Some quite clearly, and others somewhat vaguely, reject the sacerdotal approach; disbelieve the theory of the Mass; find themselves unable to get a bit of bread for their souls that way; look up, as hungry sheep, and are not fed.

In hundreds of villages in this country the only evangelical interpretation of the Gospel is in the Methodist chapel. Quite often it is the only Free Church in the hamlet and bears the immense responsibility of offering Christ (as evangelicals understand it) alone. The importance of this in the spiritual life of England could barely be exaggerated. The withdrawal of this ministry would be a calamity which few who care for spiritual things could contemplate with equanimity.

6. Nor do the unfinished tasks end even here.

There is considerable interest in the country, and in the civilized world, at present concerning the true nature of *money*. Is it simply a token, a symbol of credit, a mark in a ledger, a figment created by banks? Or does it come nearer to reality than any of these phrases suggest?

Religious people go farther in their questionings. What is the relation of money—howsoever conceived—to the work of the Church, to the maintenance of its ministry, to the spread of the Christian faith abroad? Should the vast inequalities which mark the remuneration of men in secular callings have their counterpart among men commissioned to spread the teaching of the Galilean Carpenter? Should a man's ability to present himself as called of God for that commission depend, not just on his gifts and graces, but on his ability (or that of his parents) to buy him an education which shall fit him for the task?

It is idle to say that these questions do not matter. Any man who has preached the Gospel in the open air knows that they matter very much. He is constantly having the topic thrown in his teeth. The man in the street seriously questions whether a Church subtly seduced by the standards of the world can give clear guidance to perplexed humanity on a subject so central and absorbing as this.

Yet that branch of the Church called Methodism (and notably in its British section) has an answer to these problems—so far, at least, as they concern the actual working of the Church. It is not an impracticable theory, lightly set down by some zealous pamphleteer, newly converted to the idea that money is only a symbol. It has worked for 200 years. It has had no small part in making the Methodist ministry a brotherhood as close-knit in affection and understanding as any body of men could be. It might even yet prove itself the living example of how this perplexing problem of money and the ministry might be solved and show the path by which the whole Church might find its way and lead the world.

7. Finally, Methodism has special skill in enlisting the service of laymen.

It is not given to a large number of men and women to know with intimacy the inside of two Communions, and it is one of the pains of divided Christendom that good people can live a long life in virtual ignorance of how their Christian neighbours worship and how they do the work of God.

But it is often freely said by those who make acquaintance in maturity with Methodism that they are astonished at the devotion of her laymen and the responsibilities they splendidly bear not only in the business concerns of the Church but in preaching and teaching as well.

Nor would there be any disposition to decline that compliment on the part of a Methodist minister. He has had need a thousand times to glorify God for the consecration of the laity. He looks back through the years and in circuit after circuit he can think of men from nearly all social strata giving a whole-souled devotion to our Lord. He knows men prodigal with their leisure, their money, their love, their learning, and he marvels at the privilege of serving them in holy things.

Many discerning observers believe that in the present age the laity must take the foremost place in the battle for Britain's soul. A certain cynicism infects the mind of the estranged masses toward those who have made religion their career. It can be overcome by personal acquaintance, but they are out of touch with parsons and some of them know little of the economic leanness of the minister's life. They armour themselves against the parson's most passionate evangelical appeal with the conviction that 'it's only his job'.

They cannot armour themselves against the laity like that. The simple, direct, and intensely personal witness of

THERE *IS* AN UNFINISHED TASK   21

another man working on the same bench, or in the same
office, pierces their defences. Resist it as they will, it has
a way of stabbing home.

How can we more enlist the laymen in the militant
service of our Lord? How can we make them vocal and
informed and incisive and always alert in the great
campaign of Christ?

If Methodism has any special craft in doing this
necessary and urgent task it is a skill peculiarly precious
at the present time.

Well, that is the sevenfold task as I see it: the historic
mission together with certain other specific ministries
begotten in two centuries of developing life. Let it be
said again that, in describing this as the distinctive mission
of Methodism, no suggestion is made (or could be made)
that she alone is concerned about holiness, evangelism, the
social order, reunion, rural areas, the use of money, or
the service of the laity. But it *is* claimed that she ap-
proaches each of these in a manner peculiarly her own and
is commissioned to work in a segment of the field where her
equipment is especially precious to God.

But certain teasing questions concerning each of these
specific tasks still remain. How can holiness be made
attractive? Is it suggested—even for one moment—that
Methodism strikes a note here which no other Church
contributes to the heavenly harmony?

Is her evangelism distinctive? Has she an adaptability
or a technique which is both characteristic and valuable?
Or is the mere supposition that she does possess such skill
another expression of denominational pride?

Even supposing that she did provide many of the early
leaders and martyrs of the labouring classes struggling
for justice in Britain, is it not plainly true today that

Methodism has lost the labouring classes and become a sect of the lower-middle class?

As for any special aid that she might render to reunion, do not the examples of France and Canada urge her to bury her 'distinctiveness' and merge with all speed into some larger whole?

Can the service of rural areas be seriously pleaded as a contribution to the life of Britain and the Kingdom of God? Is there not something aesthetically offensive, when one motors through the villages of our land, to see the noble parish church offset by the mean village chapel, often unbelievably ugly, and built to the same 'architecture' as a dog-kennel?

Is it remotely likely that a Church with a separate history of 200 years can teach anything about the use of money to a Communion which comes nigh to numbering its years at 2,000?

Even if we set aside those bodies of Christians which have no ordained ministry at all, can a Communion which virtually disallows a layman from presiding over a church business meeting claim any special skill in enlisting the service of laymen?

Such are the questions which now confront us. Let us examine them each in turn.

CHAPTER TWO

IN SPREADING SCRIPTURAL HOLINESS

IT GOES without saying that no one has more right to speak of God's purpose in calling Methodism into being than John Wesley. This amazing man—whose stature seems to grow with passing time—was the chief instrument in the Divine hand for raising this people up, and making them the third largest Church in England and one of the largest Protestant Churches in the world.

However unexpected, therefore, the answer Wesley might give concerning God's intention in raising the Methodists, and however quaintly his phrasing may sound in our ears, no sober student of the subject could cheerfully ignore what Wesley himself said. And he said *this* concerning the doctrine of Scriptural Holiness (sometimes called Christian Perfection, Entire Sanctification, or Perfect Love): 'This doctrine is the grand depositum which God has lodged with the people called Methodists, and for the sake of propagating this chiefly He appears to have raised us up.'

Respect for the opinion of John Wesley, therefore, demands a primacy for holiness in any consideration of Methodism's unfinished tasks.

But other considerations demand it too. If one had only the slightest interest in the opinions of the Founder of Methodism, any honest consideration of life from a religious or ethical viewpoint would bring the need of holiness swift to the forefront of one's mind. The world's poverty in holiness cries aloud to Heaven. Sin, in all its multitudinous forms, speaks out this patent lack. It is the way of zealots, peddling their own peculiar nostrum for the cure of the world's ills, to say: 'The *one* thing we need . . .', but so often they complete their sentence with some little ecclesiastical prescription which provokes nothing in us but a smile. If there is any value in reducing the world's clamant needs to this degree of singularity, then the one thing we need is *holiness*. All other needs are pendent on it. It is so central and primary that it may be said without exaggeration that if we sought and found this—all other things would be added unto us.

Consider how true this is concerning the Church.

1. It is commonly said that the Church needs *revival*. Holiness would bring revival. It was of revival that Lacordaire was thinking when he said: 'O God! give us some saints.'

That was why almost all France (with any spiritual insight at all) went to Ars in the third and fourth decades of the last century to see the most lowly born and ill-instructed priest in the country because he was a saint, and a saint can arrest a worldling. That is why many of the most discerning people among us today argue that it is not a mission we need most to the people quite estranged from the Church, but a mission to those who are inside. Holiness would bring revival.

2. Holiness would bring spiritual power. It is given by the Holy Spirit, and the Holy Spirit is also the Spirit of Power: the Lord and Giver of Life. The world could not long ignore a holy Church. It is because there is not enough difference today between the Church and the world that the former fails to be impressive, but in a Church where saints were as common as they are now rare, the difference would smite by its contrast.

3. Holiness would answer unbelief. It would not answer it by logic, and the work of the Christian philosopher would still need to be done, but it would destroy its pertness and nourish the will to venture—which is ever the essence of faith. Voltaire and Edgar Wallace—both of whom knew the underworld in their different ways, and found faith hard—found it impossible to take up their permanent abode in unbelief. They both knew a Methodist saint.[1] Saints have this sublime distinction.

---

[1] *Encyclopaedia Britannica*, Vol. IX, p. 373. Abbey and Overton, *The English Church in the Eighteenth Century*, p. 113. Margaret Lane, *Edgar Wallace*, p. 84.

They make it well-nigh impossible for other people to deny the faith.

4. Holiness is the highway to reunion. All who long and pray for the reunion of God's dismembered Church are on their guard against the people who are in such haste for this end that they believe (grotesquely enough) that the end can be achieved by further 'chopping-off'. It is a kind of unholy barter. 'If we give up this, will you give up that?' They would strip themselves (and others) of all distinctiveness, and deny, by implication, that the idiosyncrasies of personality may be as dear to God in a denomination as in an individual. The kind of Church they would make at the end might be 'one', but it would be neither 'Holy, Catholic, nor Apostolic'.

The saints would show them the way. 'Get near to the Cross and you get near to one another.' The saints of all Communions are already members of one Communion. They know each other when they meet. Deep calleth unto deep. The ecclesiastics toil and moil to get a formula —as, indeed, they must—but the saints have outsoared their labour. First the sign—and then the countersign! One glance at Keble's face convinced a bewildered Roman Catholic that there was holiness outside his Church. Few men better understood or more highly appraised the work of Dale in Birmingham (that 'unworldly man of the world') than his distinguished fellow-townsman, John Henry Newman.

It will be said, however, in comment on all this, that the importance of holiness is not in dispute, but that it was in no sense a monopoly of John Wesley's even in the England of the eighteenth century. It was partly true then, and it is certainly true now, that the concern about it, and the quest after it, is in all the Churches.

And, of course, it *is*. That is one of the glad, good things to rejoice in, even in these centuries of sad division. Strictly speaking, there are no doctrines peculiar to Methodists—as there are, for instance, to Christian Scientists and Mormons—and, if there were, they would be no part of the faith once delivered to the saints, and would be justly classified as heresies.

Rejoicing, as Methodists do, that the concern after holiness is in all Communions, they claim an emphasis in their teaching upon it, and an accent in their enunciation of it, which is unique in all the major branches of the Christian Church. They hold that their teaching is firmly set in the Scriptures but was neglected, in the evangelical understanding of it, for centuries, and that John Wesley was speaking words of truth and soberness when he said that 'for the sake of propagating this chiefly' God had raised his people up.

Can this claim be made out? If, indeed, sanctity is the great end of God for us all, and His purpose through the ages moves toward this speechless consummation; if, in the reckonings of Heaven, a saint outshines the loftiest prince, or ripest scholar, or most exquisite artist (though he might be any one of these as well)—then the emergence of sanctity is of immense importance *anywhere*, and the study of its growth and cultivation should command the attention of all reverent men. If, moreover, in adoring wonder, humble, holy men claim to have discovered in the Scriptures the source of new power for holiness, and if the claim is attested by a succession of living witnesses who file unbroken through half a dozen generations—then this witness simply cannot be ignored. It is not a denominational idiosyncrasy: it matters to the whole Church of God. It cannot be a sectarian peculiarity: it is part of the priceless treasure of Christendom.

Now, that is the claim made for John Wesley's approach

to holiness. Methodist theologians hold—while still debating aspects of the doctrine between themselves— that Wesley effected 'an original and unique synthesis of the Protestant ethic of grace with the Catholic ethic of holiness'.[1] They claim originality for Wesley here only in the sense that he first drew out what was already securely set in the Scriptures. They believe—marvelling, almost, at the audacity of their belief—that no other branch of the Church is so committed by its divine commission or standards of doctrine to this precise emphasis, and that Methodism's task will remain un- finished until all the ransomed Church of God has seen this gleaming facet of truth. They are far from thinking that this is their only task. But it is *one* task. And, as John Wesley ever put it first, they put it first themselves.

The uniqueness of Wesley's contribution to theological thought in this regard can best be drawn out by showing what need both Protestantism and Catholicism have of each other when the quest for holiness is in mind.

Disinclined as some students of Reformation theology are to admit it, it cannot honestly be doubted that Luther's teaching does not deal seriously enough with the moral problem. His own most distinguished interpreters have admitted so much.[2] His immense (and Scriptural) stress upon faith—and faith only—was left unbalanced by the lack of a complementary passion for holiness. Unwittingly, he left the door ajar to antinomianism.

Nor is it hard to see how this could happen. Underline the worthlessness of our own righteousness; emphasize the utter pollution of human nature; put it beyond hope that,

[1] G. C. Cell, *The Rediscovery of John Wesley*, p. 347. Umphrey Lee, *John Wesley and Modern Religion*, p. 190.
[2] e.g., Adolph Harnack, *History of Dogma*, Vol. VII, p. 267 (E.T.).

even by grace, one may live a day without sin in thought, word, and deed (as the Westminster Catechism does),[1] and then stress faith and faith only—and, in this world of purblind sinners, misunderstanding is sure to arise.

The misunderstandings arose. They arose, not so much from the falsity in what had been said, as from the unbalance which results from leaving much unsaid. It is plain, historical fact—grotesque as it was as an interpretation of Luther—that many claimed to be living in faith while repudiating any interest in a holy life. Indeed, their perverted theory of faith *required* them to display a certain scorn of holiness. Deep concern about right living was labelled 'pharisaism'. They called those who held it 'enemies of the Lamb'. Some of them got drunk, lapsed into lying and adultery, and defended themselves by saying: 'The Lamb shall have the honour of saving me: I will not offer to save myself like you Pharisees.'[2]

Now, Wesley had to face that situation. If it seems an academic point now, it was plain and practical then. It baffled him for a while, how it could be so: what deficient note in Protestant theology had made this caricature possible. Finally, he traced it back through his loved Moravians to a serious unbalance in Luther's theology. Wesley had been brought by the Spirit of God to his own evangelical conversion by Luther's Preface to Paul's Epistle to the Romans: now he reads Luther's *Commentary on Galatians*—and he is shaken to the depths. He describes himself as 'utterly ashamed'. He marvels 'how blasphemously' Luther speaks 'of good works and the law of God'.[3] He openly warned his congregations against the *Commentary* and turned, with deeper longing than ever,

[1] *Westminster Confession: The Larger Catechism*, Q. 149.
[2] *The Lives of Early Methodist Preachers*, Vol. I, p. 140 (Edit. 1871).
[3] *Journal*, Vol. II, p. 467.

to the Ante-Nicene fathers and the rich treasures of Catholic spirituality.

No wonder, therefore, that some in the main stream of Protestant theology came to regard Wesley as half a renegade and mistakenly assumed that he had reverted to the idea of working his passage to Heaven by accumulated good deeds. This great little man knew, in his own life-time, the bane and blessing which the denomination he unwillingly founded has known ever since: a foot in each camp: a mid-position begotten, not by irresolution, or muddled thinking, but begotten (as Wesley believed) by loyalty to the truth.

Luther's attitude to the quest for holiness has remained an influence in Protestantism ever since. It can be traced clearly through 400 years. It comes out in characteristic sayings of men like Count Zinzendorf[1] and P. T. Forsyth,[2] and explains why 'perfectionist' is a term of mild scorn among many modern Protestant theologians. Professor John Baillie rightly admits that 'the main development of Reformation thought estimates very lightly the possibility of the acquisition of holiness during this present life'.[3] Professor Reinhold Niebuhr, discussing 'the issue upon which the Protestant Reformation separated itself from classical Catholicism', argues that the peace which Paul had found in Christ must have 'moral content in it, *a fact which Reformation theology tends to deny.* . . .'[4] A militant Protestant theologian like Dr. Cadoux said: '. . . there is a special ethical intensity which, without injustice to the morals of Protestantism, may yet truthfully be predicated of the Catholic character.'[5]

[1] John Wesley, *Journal*, Vol. II, p. 490.
[2] *Christian Perfection*, pp. 12, 84, 134.
[3] *Invitation to Pilgrimage*, p. 71.
[4] *Christianity and Power Politics*, pp. 18f. (my italics).
[5] *Catholicism and Christianity*, p. 77.

The master passion of Wesley's life for thirteen years before his evangelical conversion was holiness, and deeply as he admired Luther in some ways, he could never come to terms with what he regarded as this major defect in Lutheran theology. He contended that God could do something more with sin than forgive it. To say that God can save us *in* sinning is not enough, Wesley argued: He can save us *from* sinning. Wesley believed that over-much stress upon the *imputation* of righteousness can blind us to the *impartation* of it. The plea for a little harboured sin on the ground that it keeps one humble (a plea made in every generation) is a plea he would never allow.

To Wesley it bordered on the blasphemous to set any limit to what the grace of God could do with a soul, even on this earth. No man, he believed, was equipped to come forward and say: 'God cannot do *this* . . . and will not do *that*.' To take such a view (with the New Testament open before one) seemed to the Founder of Methodism dangerously near to disbelieving God. To hold the fixed conviction in one's mind that God cannot break the power of cancelled sin and set the prisoner free, requires that one must always mentally provide for sin, and runs counter to Paul's injunction: 'Make no provision for the flesh to fulfil the lusts thereof.' The desiring heart fixes upon 'inevitability' as an ever-ready excuse, for no man can press on confidently and unswervingly to what he has already decided is utterly unattainable.

But how did Wesley defend himself in his own mind against the charge of Protestant zealots (some of whom called him a 'Papist'), that he was reverting to salvation by works and bringing his people again under the domination of a rigorous legal code? In what sense was his great preoccupation with holiness to be distinguished from that of the Catholic saints he so much admired and from the general pursuit of sanctity as practised in the Roman Church?

Wesley repudiated the double standard of morality implied in the Roman system: one for ordinary men and women and one for the 'religious'. There is but one standard for all. Holiness does not require the segregated life of the convent and the monastery for its serious pursuit. The holy life must be lived *in* the world. To refuse life is hardly less heinous than to abuse life. To use life for God where men buy and sell, sin and suffer; where babes are born and economic problems press upon the parents; where wills clash and the Christ-filled soul can serve as reconciler—*there* is the sphere of holy living as Jesus Christ Himself showed. So Charles Wesley taught his friends to sing:

> *Not in the tombs we pine to dwell,*
> *Not in the dark monastic cell,*
> *By vows and grates confined;*
> *Freely to all ourselves we give,*
> *Constrained by Jesu's love to live*
> *The servants of mankind.*[1]

But the difference is deeper than that. From much brooding in the Book of God Wesley came to believe that faith, which, on any honest scrutiny of the New Testament, is so mightily approved by God in justification, is mightily used by God in *sanctification* as well: that the way to the sublime goal is not the way of classical Catholicism— segregation, asceticism, midnight vigils, scourging, and maceration[2]—but the way of daring faith, claiming from God the gift of perfect love and being maintained in a moment-by-moment life of dependence on Him. Holiness

---

[1] *Methodist Hymn-book* (Edit. 1904), No. 599.
[2] Rome has many non-monastic saints, of course.

cannot be *achieved*, Wesley taught: it is a *gift* of God. It is given in answer to faith and can be given in a moment. It is best described as 'perfect love'. It is positive, therefore, with all the energy of love, but plainly supernatural. It does not run on lines of mere affinity: it loves where, by human nature, it could not like. Those who have this gift find that God 'is their one desire, their one delight, and they are continually happy in Him. They love their neighbour as themselves. They feel as sincere, fervent, constant a desire for the happiness of every man, good or bad, friend or enemy, as for their own. They rejoice evermore, pray without ceasing, and in everything give thanks. Their souls are continually streaming up to God, in holy joy, prayer, and praise'.[1]

Sin is mastered by this divine gift and ceases to have dominion over the adoring recipient. He is still subject to infirmity, ignorance, and mistake, but he can serve God now with a sensitive conscience, and yet a conscience void of offence. For what has been wrought in him, he gives all the glory to God, and the discerning know him by his humbling humility. He murmurs with Paul: 'We who died to sin, how shall we any longer live therein? . . . Our old man was crucified with Him, that the body of sin might be done away, that so we should no longer be in bondage to sin. . . . But now, being made free from sin, and become servants to God, we have our fruit unto sanctification.'[2]

It would be idle to deny that great controversy has raged around the explanation of this doctrine, though it can be said that there is a complete answer to most of the objections that are raised.

Any student taking up its study for the first time would

[1] *A Plain Account of Christian Perfection*, p. 90.
[2] Romans 6 [2, 6, 22].

do well never to lose sight of two things which, together, constitute the strength of this doctrine as the Methodists understand it: first, the whole thing is flung back upon God and, secondly, the stress falls not on difficult definitions of 'perfection' or on academic discussions of the *summum bonum*, but on the need ever to keep the supreme goal in view.

And this, at least, is incontrovertible. When serious theologians claim that Wesley made 'an original and unique synthesis of the Protestant ethic of grace with the Catholic ethic of holiness', they are saying something of major importance.

It is of major importance in Methodism itself. One of the tragedies of this branch of the Church is to be found in her neglect of the very doctrine God raised her up to recover. It is not understood, seldom preached, half hidden by some (who apologize when they mention it) and left, alas! to people who have been labelled (justly or unjustly) as 'cranks'.

Many ministers in Methodism do not even esteem the doctrine as a treasure, and would part from it without pain. When they hear that a considerable theologian of another Communion—like Dr. R. W. Dale of Birmingham—spoke of this teaching with profound respect but marvelled at the 'want of the genius or the courage' to develop in Methodism the treasure which Wesley had left—they are mildly interested but not obviously eager to provide 'the genius or the courage' he called for. Many of the more thoughtful ministers of Methodism are drawn—as well they may be in some ways—to the Neo-Calvinist school in theology, but do not seem (so far as my observation goes) to be sufficiently aware of all that was involved in the clash between Methodism and Calvinism in the eighteenth century, nor the extent of the victory their spiritual fathers won.

These new allegiances may cost them more than they know. At least, they should see with clear eyes what this shift in emphasis involves, and how it may lead them definitely away from the historic mission of their Church. 'The main development of Reformation thought', we have been reminded, 'estimates very lightly the possibility of the acquisition of holiness during this present life.' Methodism estimates it very highly. 'That there must be and there is moral content in the peace a Christian enjoys in Christ is', we have been informed, 'a fact which Reformation theology tends to deny.' It is a fact which Methodism would die to affirm. When Dr. Cadoux said that Protestantism is inferior 'in a special ethical intensity which . . . may yet truthfully be predicated of the Catholic character', he had to be understood as describing the Protestantism he knew best. Methodists, at least, would want to add this: 'We are committed by our very standards to keep an immense stress on holiness. God forgive us if our friends and neighbours are unaware of it, but we are not truly ourselves when the emphasis is not there.'

Maybe this is the explanation of the fact that there has often been a penetrating understanding of Methodists by Roman Catholics, and of Roman Catholics by Methodists: why, for instance, a Franciscan friar like Professor Maximin Piette could write with such amazing insight of John Wesley,[1] and why such characteristic Methodists as Samuel Chadwick[2] and A. E. Whitham should feed with such naturalness and nourishment in the wide fields of Catholic spirituality. Despite the failures of both Communions—and what branch of Christ's Church fully lives up to its own ideals?—a burning vision of sanctity beckons alike these pilgrims on.

Here, then, is a unique ministry for Methodism in the

[1] *John Wesley in the Evolution of Protestantism.*
[2] N. Dunning, *Samuel Chadwick.*

fellowship of the Protestant Church. Her theological
position in regard to holiness is definitely different in its
emphasis from all other major branches among the
Reformed Communions. It may be said humbly, but
quite positively, that the truth of God would suffer if this
emphasis were lost. God does not continue to bless with
His grace, and furnish with saints, a Communion of fifty
million souls, if it is not dear to His heart and matched to
its task.

But how much is Methodism matched to its task?—how
conscious are her sons and daughters of the mission they
share with all faithful believers and the mission peculiarly
their own?—how concerned are they even to understand
intelligently the precious part of their heritage we have discussed in this chapter? Why was it that only in her overseas
work did the advance continue, and year after year, in the
country which cradled world Methodism, her forces
fell back? Is the Spirit of God saying to this Church:
'Remember, therefore, from whence thou art fallen, and
repent, and *do the first works:* or else I will come unto thee
quickly, and remove thy candlestick out of his place'?[1]

Years ago, I went on a pilgrimage to Holy Island. When
I reached the spot on the Northumbrian coast from which
it is usual for pilgrims to strike out, at low water, across
the sands, I noticed a garage, eager to save travellers the
exertion and the risk. The garage proprietor had
marshalled a fleet of old cars by which the two-mile
journey to the home of St. Aidan and St. Cuthbert could
be made with speed and almost with comfort. He
announced his service, on a large notice-board, thus:

VISIT HOLY ISLAND!

TREAD WHERE THE SAINTS HAVE TROD.

WE CAN TAKE YOU!

[1] Revelation 2 [5].

It seemed to me then, and it seems to me still, a challenge to the Church to which I belong. Every branch of Christ's Church, one may assume, has its own song to contribute to the swelling harmonies of Heaven, and men of catholic mind delight to notice and cherish the lovely melodies which others sing. A chief part of Methodism's distinctive song concerned the Way of Holiness. She does not sing it now as well as once she did. Is it too much to hope that she will do again her 'first works' and turn to the people of this country, drifting into paganism, and say:

> Tread where the saints have trod
> We can take you?

CHAPTER THREE

IN EVANGELIZING THE WORLD-PARISH

It CAN BE said without fear of contradiction that no branch of the Christian Church denies the duty of evangelism. All have taken heed of Our Lord's solemn and final admonition: 'Go ye, therefore, and make disciples of all the nations.'

Nevertheless, it is not unfair to say that the primacy and urgency of evangelism is variously estimated among Christians, and in the methods of evangelism the widest differences prevail.

In some branches of the Church the main stress appears to be placed on the spiritual nurture of the children of the Communion. 'If the flock is shepherded,' the reasoning appears to run, 'the future is secure. A well-instructed and devout body of believers will make its own impression on the community, and proselytes will come in of their own desire. No special appeal in public meetings or in the open air to masses of the unchurched multitude is either necessary or wise.'

What is called the 'cell' method is warmly commended elsewhere. Sharing the growing distaste that is widely felt for 'popular' evangelistic services, those who suggest the 'cell' method insist that it is the method of the New Testament. Men and women are converted to God. All life becomes new for them. They can no more keep the new life to themselves than a lover can conceal the light in his eye. They speak of it to others; form a circle of those who seek and then secure the experience; encourage the new converts to form a cell of their own—and on and on it goes. 'That is the way of evangelism,' say these earnest advocates. 'It avoids all the dangers of mass meetings and emotional appeals. Most of all, it avoids that fatal confusion between the longing for a higher quality of life (which is common to all men) and an actual work of grace wrought in the heart by the Spirit of God. So many people who respond to public appeals to "come to Christ" are only registering "desire" and it is the recurrent sin of the mass evangelist that he identifies "to want" and "to have".'

But is any 'crisis' in the spiritual life necessary at all? That is the question which other Christians who would certainly claim to be concerned about evangelism constantly raise. The old distinction between the 'once born' and the 'twice born' is ever in their mind. At the risk of appearing to contradict the New Testament they contest the belief that it is necessary to pass through the experience which evangelicals describe as being 'born again'. 'The thought of the Church is too Augustinian,' they argue. To impose the dramatic experience of quite unusual men like Paul, Augustine, Luther, and Wesley on the mass of mankind is utterly mistaken: it ignores deep differences of temperament. And to confine one's ideas of evangelism to the effort to create this crisis in the heart of all men and women is mistaken in theory and will most certainly fail in practice. Its fatal flaw, as Charles Williams believes, is here: its advocates never seem 'quite to apprehend that a man could grow, sweetly and naturally—and no less naturally and sweetly in spite of all the stages of repentance necessarily involved—from man into new man'.[1]

Yet it needs hardly to be said that those who reject the Augustinian approach would resent the suggestion that they are not evangelists. There are many ways to Christ, they remind us, and more people become aware of the new day by the slow breaking of the dawn than by any sudden step from total darkness into blinding light.

Not a few who reject the rigidity of the 'born-again' beginning put stress on the essential, if latent, goodness in ordinary men and women and seek, by the creation of a Christian community life, to get people 'free' in their own environment and, without talk of God or Christ or worship, to draw them into a fellowship outside the Churches which is, nevertheless, full of the presence of Christ and in which (it is hoped) they will slowly come to know their place in the universe and to believe in the reality and love of God.[2]

The weight of opinion in the Christian Church seems to have turned decisively against mass evangelism and is turning now against 'popular' services.

The word 'popular' is awkward to define in this connexion, but it may be characterized as non-liturgical worship, warm, with plenty of congregational singing, and preaching which keeps close to life. It is, in short, worship

[1] *The Descent of the Dove*, p. 64.
[2] cf. Joseph McCulloch, *Medway Adventure*.

as commonly offered in Methodism and in most of the
other Free Churches. Even within the Communions where
this form of service is characteristic, criticism is constantly
offered of it, and the Church of England is noticing with
interest the growth of liturgical worship among Nonconformists.[1]

'Free' worship is felt to depend too much upon the
minister himself. Nearly everything is left to him. His
ideas, his convictions, even his prejudices and his moods
shadow the whole service: even the prayers.

The service is said to have no wholeness and unity.
The different parts of worship follow each other like
unrelated 'items': there is no building up or climax:
people come, it is suggested, mainly to hear the sermon
which is treated, therefore, as a superior form of entertainment: everything before it is just 'preliminary'.

Extemporary prayer is felt by these critics to be
peculiarly distasteful. Even friendly Anglicans tell us
affectionately that it 'makes them shudder'. The idea
of addressing the Deity with a minimum of thought and
just opening the mouth and saying what comes is almost
irreverent. When it isn't irreverent—and a devout heart
will secure it from that—it still isn't *corporate* prayer.

People cannot follow quickly enough the changes in
the minister's thought in extemporary prayer. To pray
together all must know what is coming next. The
identification of the self with the prayer which is proffered
takes more time than continuous speech allows. Consequently, when extemporary prayer is part of public
worship, the people listen to *one* person praying, snatching
perhaps a phrase here and there to which in their hearts
they attach an unspoken and hasty 'Amen'.

If, to these other defects, is added a selection of sentimental hymns, no moments left for real silence and a

[1] G. W. Ireson, *Church Worship and the Non-Churchgoer*, p. 62.

hearty gusto interpenetrating all—well, it might be
many things, but it falls far short of any high ideal of
worship.

Liturgical worship is said to be the answer to all this.
'The Church', we are told, 'lives by dogma and liturgy.'[1]
The whole service is planned and the people know what is
coming. The service is *shared*: minister and congregation
are bound up in it. It has progression and unity. Three
hymns are felt to be enough.[2] Fifteen minutes is suggested
for the sermon.[3]

Not a few Free Church ministers have been convinced
of all this and are experimenting with liturgies. I am
bound to say that their efforts—so far as I have experience
of them—fall far below the level of the Book of Common
Prayer, but in explanation of their practice they confess
that their extemporary prayer was only extemporary in
name. In point of fact they had found themselves
repeating the same outworn phrases over and over again,
and they felt it was more devout carefully to write out
their prayers and read them, or employ the words of
ancient liturgies sanctified by generations of common
use.

In an age when the 'free' form of worship seems to be
falling into disfavour I want to utter a word in its defence.

To begin with, there is no reason at all why non-
liturgical worship (as the Rev. G. W. Ireson seems to
think) is less able to sustain dogma than the liturgical
form.[4] So far as the preaching is concerned the sermon
can be 'a dose of uplift' rather than the proclamation of
the eternal gospel in either mode of worship.

Nor is it necessary for the free form of worship to be a

[1] G. W. Ireson, op. cit., p. 6.
[2] ibid., p. 158.
[3] *Theology*, Vol. XIX, p. 19; but cf. p. 21.
[4] G. W. Ireson, op. cit., pp. 5f., cf. p. 60; cf. also A. G. Hebert, *Liturgy
and Society*.

mere succession of unrelated 'items'. I am bold to say
that when it is under the direction of an instructed minister
of God that is precisely what it is not. In such hands,
the service has plan and progression. In the Free Churches
—and most certainly among the Methodists—the hymn-
book is the prayer-book of the people. That is why four
or even five hymns are not too many.

It would surprise Christians unused to non-liturgical
services what care a minister, skilled in this mode of
worship, takes over the choice of his hymns. How careful
he is not to have all his hymns on one theme. How
concerned that adoration, confession, intercession, have
their place on the people's lips as well as on his own. How
plainly he can guide them in the mere act of announcing
the hymn by a simple prefatory phrase: 'A hymn of
praise . . .' or: 'Let us pray for missions abroad as we
sing hymn number . . .' or: 'Dedicate yourselves anew
to God in this final hymn of consecration. . . .' It would
be a vulgar mistake to suppose that hymns in this form of
worship are chosen haphazardly, the main idea being
to 'let the people have a good sing'.

No one acquainted with the hymns of Charles Wesley
and aware that they are still the main staple of Methodist
hymnology would ever suggest that the characteristic
songs of this people are sentimental effusions. Many of
Charles Wesley's hymns—most of them—are of doctrine
all compounded. Scripture is woven into their very tex-
ture. Taken together, they form a compact body of
divinity. The constant use of these hymns is a chief way
in which the Methodist people learn their theology. If
occasional use is made in their services of inferior hymns
born in the mass evangelism of the later nineteenth century,
it can never be called their characteristic song and only
registers the rightful recognition that if simple souls are
helped by this quality of hymnology it should not be

firmly denied them. With passing time, they learn to love the better thing.

It was Bernard Manning, Fellow and Tutor of Jesus College, Cambridge, and a considerable authority on hymns, who, speaking from outside the Methodist fold, said of the original *Methodist Hymn-book*:

> You may think my language about the hymns extravagant: therefore I repeat it in stronger terms. This little book . . . ranks in Christian literature with the Psalms, the Book of Common Prayer, the Canon of the Mass. In its own way, it is perfect, unapproachable, elemental in its perfection. You cannot alter it except to mar it; it is a work of supreme devotional art by a religious genius. You may compare it with Leonardo's 'Last Supper' or King's Chapel; and, as Blackstone said of the English Constitution, the proper attitude to take to it is this: we must venerate where we are not able presently to comprehend.[1]

Nor is extempory prayer so hard to make corporate as liturgiologists may suppose.

It is—as one may freely admit—the most costing part of the service to the minister. To preach is easy in comparison.

Because the prayer is not verbally prepared, it would be mistaken to suppose that no preparation goes to it. One prepares *oneself*. Who that bears this awful responsibility of standing between God and men in the conduct of free public worship but knows the discipline of spirit this preparation requires; the spiritual identification of oneself with the people in all the variety of their need; the divesting oneself *of* oneself lest the subjective intrude at the mercy-seat; the overpowering sense of 'priesthood' as one prepares to speak for all—and, at the last, that inward

[1] *The Hymns of Wesley and Watts*, p. 14.

word from God to go and lead His people to His presence? And who, in this succession, does not know also the equipment He gives for the task and for which I can use no other word than the out-moded word 'unction'— soiled though it is by satirical misuse?

We used to speak in the Free Churches of certain people who had 'the gift of prayer'. They seem to be fewer now than they were. But they were unmistakable. It wasn't eloquence, or felicity in phrasing, or a logical sequence in thought, or poetry in expression. It was just—the gift of prayer.

Obscure souls they often were but with many of the marks of sanctity upon them, and when they opened their mouths to pray it was without book, or stored memories of ancient liturgies, or 'fine' phrasing. But it was that 'blessed unction from above'.

> *Heaven came down our souls to greet*
> *And glory crowned the mercy-seat.*

God forgive us that this gift He is so ready to bestow we have not all more diligently sought.

But we know it is there to be had. And it belongs to our tradition in a way which liturgies can never do. And to seek it and use it is part of our Free Church contribution to reunited Christendom.

It will not be supposed from this that there is opposition to liturgical worship as such in Methodism. We are free to worship in the way that we wish. The Anglican service of Holy Communion, with few changes, is still ours and has been in our unbroken use for more than 200 years. In many Methodist churches the Anglican form of morning prayer is the established and cherished form of worship for the first service of the day and the Book of Offices is liturgical throughout.

But the problem which faces all keen Christians in these islands is how we can win our unchurched fellow-countrymen to a recognition of God's rule in their lives and to an eagerness for worship, and I am compelled to say that I do not believe that the liturgical form of worship is the one most calculated to attract them. Indeed, Mr. Ireson, in his plea for liturgy, states frankly that 'it is inherently impossible to design a form of worship which will at one and the same time "attract" the average modern man and provide a framework in which the authentic Christian Gospel can be preached'.

His solution of the dilemma is to form—if possible—a catechumenate—an instruction class—in which interested people can be prepared for liturgical worship to which they can be invited when they are able to understand what it means.

But the task still remains to get them into the catechumenate.

I contest the statement that 'it is inherently impossible to design a form of worship which will at one and the same time "attract" the average modern man and provide a framework in which the authentic Christian Gospel can be preached'. Difficult it may be, but not 'inherently impossible'.

It is no part of the purpose of earnest Christians today to 'play off' one form of worship against another. We are all too concerned about the general drift from the Church to want to score debating points. Both the gravity and urgency of the situation, and the love which we have for each other in Christ, constrains us simply to ask how we can win the people to worship again. And we are ready, no doubt, to learn from each other.

My honest insistence is this: that with the mass of plain people today the non-liturgical service at its best gives us the best chance.

I imply no criticism of liturgies in saying that. I was bred in them. On the rare occasions when I share now in the services of the Book of Common Prayer they move me deeply, and although I suspect that there is something of nostalgia in that, the unity of the whole service and the nobility of the language will not be denied.

But that has something to do also with the rarity of the experience. When they were 'my meat day and night', and every Sunday brought the same unvarying sequence, I confess to being often overpowered by boredom. I fell to wondering why it had always to be precisely the same. Was it originally done—as I have heard suggested— because the common people couldn't read but might be expected to learn by rote what they heard every seventh day? And if that was true, why was the rule continued when only the mentally deficient were defeated by a printed page?

We may leave all that aside. The question which still confronts us is this. Yearning over the vast majority of our fellow-countrymen estranged from the Church, do we believe that a service rigidly liturgical—even at its best —is more likely to arrest and hold them than the form of worship which we have described as 'free'?

One must speak of the people one knows. My own conviction concerning the seventy per cent or eighty per cent of the folk in our land who are said never to attend any church is that liturgy confuses them: they fumble for their place in the book and are embarrassed at their inability to find it: intoning impresses them as unreal (in what we want to be the most real of all ex-periences), and not only unreal but almost unmanly. And the 'higher' the services get, the more the common people are left behind.

In those Communions which keep the firmest grip of their children and instruct them in the theory which lies behind an elaborate ritual, a dutiful attendance may be commanded and the act of worship followed with understanding.

But think of the crowds we meet at football matches, the masses of people who sprawl over the beaches of the popular sea-side resorts on summer Sundays, the plain, ordinary, decent, but God-neglecting folk of this land—the free form of worship I am persuaded gives us the better chance with them.

It is the solemn duty of most of us who are in this tradition to make the highest use of it we can. It may, of course, be cheapened and vulgarized and made altogether unworthy of its awesome purpose.

But so may liturgies! To hear the noblest and oldest prayers either droned or bleated is a pain increased rather than lessened by the dignity native to the words themselves.

We delight as Methodists in wishing well to all who love our Lord and we know that God delights in sincere adoration, howsoever it is offered. We know He is to be found in the silent assemblies of the Quaker people and we know He draws near to those who swing the censer and move in stately procession.

But we know He draws near to us also, as to our spiritual fathers: that in our simple, happy and, at times, exuberant worship (which surely becomes those who are full of the joy of the Lord) adoration over-arches all else and we are truly lost in wonder, love, and praise.

Adopting and adapting other forms of worship as we may, I hope we shall ever see the preciousness of what we have: a form of worship flexible, able to attract and hold the plain people and peculiarly serviceable in an age when most English folk are uninstructed in Christian worship altogether.

But is this mode of worship not only attractive but able to provide 'a framework in which the authentic Christian Gospel can be preached'?

Well used, I believe it is.

In the nature of the case, when people not fully convinced of the Christian faith are drawn to public worship, there must be something of mental reservation in prayer and praise and petition.

They hardly know, many of them, where they are. They are not sure, most of them, *what* they believe.

But something has drawn them and they are in the midst of a believing congregation and the Holy Spirit wraps them round.

Preaching is the big opportunity with them. Bewildering as many people find it to believe, the foolishness of preaching is a chief means God has ordained for the saving of men.

The fashionable belittling of preaching (even within the Church) explains something of the religious paralysis of the times. The supposition that people don't want it, or want it short, or want it shallow, is all false. When *The Times Literary Supplement* discussed a few years ago the problem of empty pews,[1] the anonymous layman who spoke for the church-neglecting multitude insisted that they were not 'complacent materialists'. His positive contribution to the discussion was a plea for *preaching*. What disappointed folk in attending church, he believed, were the sermons: not because they were 'too long' or gave offence, but because they were 'too scanty', did 'not strike deep enough', and were 'too conciliatory and timid'. He deprecated too much topicality in preaching and the treatment of themes in the manner of 'leader-writers or politicians or merchants'. He was sure the layman would never be held by a preacher who played

[1] 7th October 1944, et seq.

down to him, but he saw the solution of the empty pews in the preacher 'who, fearlessly and without compromise, referred his subject, whatever it may be, to the innermost truths of Christianity'.

For preachers to disparage preaching—even if they prefer to call themselves priests—is truly Gilbertian. To protest that one has no intention of sinking into a popular preacher (with the modest implication that, of course, it would be easy if one wished!) hardly deceives a soul. To dismiss the plea of the laity for more and deeper preaching by the assertion 'that it is a priest's duty to feed the sheep rather than amuse the goats'[1] is not dealing seriously with the situation.

Those 'goats' are the sheep for whom Christ died. If preaching can be made attractive, interesting, instructive, and carry its due freight of doctrinal truth, a double duty will be done. The faithful will be nourished and the seekers will be drawn nearer home.

It is the delusion of incompetents that popular preaching must necessarily be cheap and thin. The truth is rather that a low quality of preaching does not continue to hold people. Our fellow countrymen are not morons. Dale, and Liddon, and F. W. Robertson, and Hugh Price Hughes, and Alexander Whyte were all (in their different ways) popular preachers. What pert critic will come forward and cast aspersions on these princes of the pulpit?

Not that power in preaching belongs only to the unusual genius. If the Christian Church could have influence with the people only on the assumption that every pulpit was filled by a man of outstanding eloquence we might well despair.

No such inference need be drawn. The diligent

[1] *The Times*, 16th September 1944.

pastor, shepherding his people but rigidly fencing enough time in every busy week for fresh preparation for the pulpit, and setting out to answer the gnawing questions on religion which seem to be latent in the hearts of all men, will win respect from a growing number of hearers. And if—in his eagerness to do the work of an evangelist—he pays especial heed to the difficulties of those who find faith hard, and, in addition to his central core of doctrinal preaching grapples (assuming he has the mental equipment) with the problems normally dealt with in the philosophy of religion, he will find the doubters especially grateful and have a greater chance with the *men*.

In my contacts with people outside the Churches I have not found them disinterested in religion. But they have endured another awful war, and Nature wears at times a God-denying look, and for all her great pretensions the Christian Church seems half-impotent in the world, and the plain man asks himself again: 'Is there a God? Does He care? Is prayer any use? What do people mean by religious *experience*?'

It may be said that any person still at this stage is certainly not ready for Christian *worship*—and that, in a sense, is true.

But they should be welcomed to it, nevertheless, and, if possible, attracted by it. The vast majority of people who neglect Church are not convinced atheists. Many of them half believe: more of them *want* to believe.

The atmosphere of devout worship is itself a converting medium. To affirm, therefore, that 'it is inherently impossible to design a form of worship which will at one and the same time "attract" the average modern man and provide a framework in which the authentic Christian Gospel can be preached' seems to me a dangerous overstatement. It is that very thing this age and land need. I believe that in the free and flexible form of worship at its best that hard thing can be done.

And this is evangelism as our Methodist fathers understood it. Not special missions conducted by itinerant evangelists—greatly used though they have been at times. But the local church itself in its normal activity reaching out to the unheeding multitude with the offer of Christ.

John Wesley didn't refer to the unevangelized as 'goats' seeking entertainment. He cared enough to go to them—the churches being closed to him—in the open air. He 'consented to be more vile' in a brickyard in Bristol on 2nd April 1739, and ended that ministry of the streets and fields under a tree in Winchelsea more than fifty years later.

It is sometimes said that his task was easier than ours because people in the eighteenth century had a sense of sin. I believe that to be exaggerated. I question whether the drunken, debased people he struggled with had any more sense of sin than the people who ignore us today.

John Wesley *created* the sense of sin—or (as we believe) the Holy Spirit did through him.

There is no mystery about his evangelical strategy.[1] He preached the law of God first. He stirred the torpid consciences of his hearers with the *demands* of God and made the glorious Gospel offer only when distressed souls, convinced of sin, wondered what they must do to be saved.

Offering the Gospel to people with no sense of need comes dangerously near to casting pearls before swine. Wesley's strategy still has much to commend it. Conscience is blunted but not dead in these people we have most in mind.

[1] *John Wesley's Letters*, Vol. III, pp. 79ff.

And what is the so-called 'cell' method but Wesley's class-meeting barely changed? These methods in evangelism are not mutually exclusive but complementary: they were complementary in Methodism's spacious days, and they can be made complementary again.

Meanwhile, the vast unevangelized mass of people in this country present the greatest opportunity to whomsoever will take it.

When I was in Eire I was astonished to learn that there was really no 'unchurched' mass of people in the sense that we understand the term here. Although there is in that country no religion 'by law established', 92.6 per cent of the people are Roman Catholic; and that means that though a man might be neglectful of his church duties and even leading a dissolute life, he is normally under the eye of a priest who carries definite pastoral responsibility for him, and a Methodist minister can hardly go to that man without the guilty feeling that he is proselytizing in a way from which most ministers would shrink.[1]

If it doesn't sound almost too 'Irish' there is nothing that our grand brethren in Eire more envy us than the millions of unchurched people to whom we may and must go with the offer of Christ—no one daring to say us 'nay'.

The people in this country are not much interested in denominationalism, or impressed by 'establishment'. Their love can be won by any Christian minister who loves them. Canon Leonard Hodgson is of opinion that only the *established* religion of a land can be called the conscience of the country and 'only an established Church

[1] I do not admit in stating this that we have no mission in Roman Catholic lands. Among the multitudes of non-practising Roman Catholics there are not a few reaching out for the evangel.

is in a position to be prophetic'.[1] Free Church ministers
will be unimpressed by that. The only time in living
memory when 'conscience' became prominent in political controversy it was 'the *Nonconformist* Conscience'—
a phrase which meant more on the lips of Hugh Price
Hughes than simple opposition to gambling and drink.

Every branch of the Church bears responsibility for
evangelism. God hasten the day when we shall shoulder
that responsibility as one undivided Church.

But while that day tarries let the followers of John
Wesley remember the especial purposes for which they
were called into being and place chief among those
purposes their duty to reclaim the lost.

CHAPTER FOUR

IN CHANGING THE SOCIAL ORDER

THE MAJORITY of Methodists, whenever they refer to
the 'traditions' of their Church, refer to the traditions of
Wesleyan Methodism. It is not altogether surprising.
Those traditions are older and, in some ways, weightier
than those of other Methodist Churches, but the easy
assumption that there were no other traditions is a source
of natural irritation to the people who have their roots
in other branches of Methodism.

Not only is it a source of irritation to a minority: it is
in certain respects, an impoverishment to all. I hope it
will offend no one when I say that, having regard to its
size, and prior to the time of Hugh Price Hughes, there
can be little question that the Primitive Methodist

---

[1]*Cambridge Review,* 10th October 1942, p. 12; cf C. Smyth, *Religion and
Politics,* pp. 10ff., and M. B. Reckitt, *The Christian in Politics,* pp. 82ff.

Church did more to aid the working man in his struggle for better conditions of labour and a living wage than the parent body itself.

Dr. G. M. Trevelyan, in his *English Social History*, pays a fitting tribute to the work of Wesley, and adds this: 'The coincidence in time of Wesley and the Industrial Revolution had profound effects upon England for generations to come.'[1]

Undoubtedly it had! No one reading the history of the English people with a mind for moral and spiritual matters but must be grateful that when that vast industrial change came over this rural land there was a mighty religious movement in full flood. As the people migrated from village to town; as new towns sprang up; as the gaunt factories with their belching chimneys stole the rustic loveliness from county after county, England may be glad that her people, experiencing the awful drudgery of mine and mill, and largely neglected by the regular clergy, had the offer of light and love and warmth and joy held out to them in Jesus Christ. The Methodist preachers did not penetrate everywhere, but nearly everywhere, and they took a peculiarly tight hold on the industrial north and west. Though Wesley's converts included some people of 'quality', the people who responded to him were drawn, for the most part, from the unprivileged masses. He repeated the experience of St. Paul: 'Not many wise after the flesh, not many mighty, not many noble, are called.'[2] These were the people most likely to be affected by the unrest of the times; most prone to feel that the industrial revolution needed to be matched by another revolution; most likely (inspired by what they heard from France) to put up revolutionary barricades and begin.

[1] p. 362.   [2] 1 Corinthians 1 26.

Those barricades were never put up in England. Several reputable historians have given Wesley the credit for the people's steadiness and restraint, and although it is probably an exaggeration to say that Wesley saved England from bloody revolution,[1] there can be no doubt that the statement has a kernel of truth.

For John Wesley was a Tory and his immense influence over the Methodist people made them profoundly conservative, too. He believed in the king and the unreformed constitution. Though he makes occasional critical comments on the social conditions of his times, and his passion to help the poor ill-assorted with his Toryism, it did not lead him to challenge, even in thought, the settled order of things.

Democracy was no object of admiration to the founder of Methodism. The people, in his view of things, ought to obey their betters. He believed that democracy and republicanism and infidelity were all bound up with one another (and in those days they often were), and he meant his people to have as little truck with the one as with the other.

News of the worst horrors of the French Revolution did not reach England until after Wesley had passed away, but his own iron conservatism was imbued in the people he had called into being, and through them it affected the classes who might most easily have been disturbed.

There were, of course, unfortunate consequences of this conservative bent.

The world has long since learned that one can be a democrat without being a republican, and most certainly without being an unbeliever. There were Methodists who took that view even in Wesley's day, but

[1] Maldwyn Edwards, *This Methodism*, pp. 35ff.

Methodism was an inhospitable home to them. The system of Church policy which Wesley had hammered out was hierarchical and (in its political sense) aristocratic. The wholly clerical Conference had all the power there was, though it was democratic within itself. Long years were to go by before laymen were even admitted to its sessions. The handful of men who swayed Conference could rule the whole denomination and completely ignore what the common people thought.

Dr. Adam Clarke said about 1819: 'The Constitution is good: it is the best under the sun: it can scarcely be mended.'[1]

This!—thirteen years before the first Reform Bill and forty-eight years before the second!! When, in the passing of time, the Conference came under the domination of the towering Dr. Jabez Bunting, whose sharp invective bludgeoned many a good man into silence and obscurity, it was inevitable that strife should arise and secession follow.

Some who left—as their subsequent history proved—were no loss at all, but others were of the salt of the earth, and only the knowledge that they went on with God can console the student of this sad chapter of Methodist history.

Perhaps nothing can better illustrate how completely out of touch official Methodism had become with its poorer people than the oft-told story of the Tolpuddle Martyrs.

It is no ordinary joy the modern Methodist experiences when he remembers that his people were among the first conspicuously to suffer in the long battle for a living wage. The six agricultural labourers of Dorset—good, God-fearing, devout men—who banded themselves together that they might increase their scandalously low

---

[1] J. W. Etheridge, *Life of Adam Clarke*, p. 311.

wages were men alive to the truth of religion and they derived their sense of social injustice from the Methodism to which five of them belonged. 'Seven shillings a week is not enough,' they said, and they got seven years' transportation for saying so. Torn from wife and child: torn from home and kin. The injustice of it cried to heaven, but—one is ashamed to set it down—official Methodism took no heed. Those gallant men went to the hulks bound for Botany Bay, but the leaders of their Church raised no hand. Strangers espoused their cause and turned night into day to get them released. The great remote Conference of Methodism utterly ignored them.

No wonder some of the finest spirits severed themselves from the main stem of Methodism and concluded that no social and political progress was possible for poor people if this attitude prevailed. Brother quarrelled with brother. Wounding things were said both ways. Reading the sad record, one can only marvel again at the bitterness of Christians in conflict.

But strip the anger away! Ignore the spleen on both sides! Honestly inquire what the controversy was over, and who can doubt that the men who challenged the authority of that dictatorial clique—and of one man in particular—were right? The things they argued and pleaded and suffered for have all been long since won. A public gallery at Conference; the laity sharing responsibility in the Church; connexional committees properly elected; the right of the Methodist people to memorialize Conference; evangelism to discover what effective forms of expression it could.

To suppose that the subsequent history of these Methodists in separation, whether as the Primitive Methodists or the Methodist New Connexion or as the United Methodist Free Church, is no part of the traditions of the reunited Church is absurd—and most absurd when one thinks on the changes in the social order of England.

Lord Passfield, writing of one aspect of progress in one area of our land, pays a glowing tribute to Durham Methodism which could be applied with equal force in other areas as well.   He says:

> No one can doubt—it would, indeed, be hard to over-estimate—the enormous improvement which has been wrought by the Methodists in their century of persistent effort in all parts of the country. Family after family became transformed, to serve in its turn as a centre of helpful influence. It is these men who, in the mining villages, have stood out as men of character, gaining the respect of their fellows. From the very beginning of the Trade Union Movement among the miners . . . and of the later attempts at Adult Education, it is men who are Methodists, and in Durham County especially the local preachers of the Primitive Methodists, whom we find taking the lead and filling the posts of influence.[1]

The controlling power in Wesleyan Methodism was to remain conservative for several decades to come, but Methodism in other forms had crept close to the workers and was to give them the leaders they needed for three generations.

What was there in Methodism that made the plain people respond to it? How came it to be so powerful an influence in the social progress of the poor?

The reason is not far to seek.

Little as the Tory in John Wesley may have realized it, the urge to democracy and the means to its achievement were all latent in the Gospel he had faithfully proclaimed and the system he had skilfully wrought.

[1] Sidney Webb, *The Story of the Durham Miners*, pp. 22f.

It was an *individual* message he had brought: it was the Gospel! The preciousness of every human soul in God's sight was gloriously stressed. The 'outcasts of men' to whom he called were made to believe that they were separately known and altogether dear to God. The personal realization which had come to him in his hour of illumination in Aldersgate Street ('an assurance was given unto me that He had taken away *my* sins, even *mine*, and saved *me* from the law of sin and death') he passed on to 'harlots, and publicans, and thieves' and to vast numbers of ordinary decent people. He taught them to stand before their God and say '*me*'.

They mattered! They mattered to God! Their status in Heaven made the over-stressed distinctions of earth a trifle to mention. They even sang:

> On all the kings of earth
> With pity we look down.

It was dynamite!—especially in the world of class distinctions prevailing in England in the eighteenth century. It would take only time to work itself out. The essential democracy latent in the timeless Gospel Wesley brought was mightier far than his personal prejudices through which he was on occasion merely a son of his own class and age.

People began to think; to assert themselves; to contrast the equality which belonged to the Gospel (and which already they enjoyed in their class-meetings) with the inequalities and injustices of social life—and a ferment began which nothing could arrest.

Add to this the technique which Wesley had developed and it isn't hard to see that the tools were at hand to undertake the task of social emancipation. The rigorous training in public speaking which every local preacher received—and the opportunity to exercise his gift. The organization of members into 'classes' and the weekly contribution of money—which the Chartists were glad to copy.[1]

It was all there. In Wesleyan Methodism the conservative element, grown wealthy with the years and altogether middle-class in outlook, maintained itself in vigour, but in the seceding bodies of Methodists the sympathy and endeavour were almost entirely with the working man. That is how the Hammonds do Methodism less than justice when they argue that the influence of Methodism was opposed to social progress because the followers of John Wesley preached contentment while the real progressives urged the people to fight for economic freedom.[2] The quotation of official Conference resolutions—damning evidence though it is—is the citation of the opinion of an entirely clerical body led largely by reactionaries and ignores both the other branches of Methodism and a vigorous minority in Wesleyan Methodism itself.

It has often been said that many of the leaders of the Labour Movement were cradled in Methodism. The list is an impressive one. Drawn from all branches of the Methodist family, they include Joseph Arch, Thomas Burt, John Wilson, Henry Broadhurst, Barnet Kenyon, W. E. Harvey, Arthur Henderson, Philip Snowden, Jack Lawson, George Isaacs, Ellen Wilkinson, George Tomlinson, etc. Methodism fortunately has never become entirely committed to one political theory or party. The common identification of Nonconformity and Liberalism, which is often made of the last decades of the nineteenth century and the first of the twentieth, was false so far as Wesleyan

[1] Maldwyn Edwards, *This Methodism*, pp. 23f.
[2] J. L. and B. Hammond, *The Town Labourer, 1760-1832*, pp. 277-87.

Methodism was concerned. It was, and is, in no sense rare to find men convinced Methodists and convinced Conservatives too (one thinks of Sir John Randles, Sir H. Kingsley Wood, and Sir Peter Bennett), but the trend of the Communion in its political influence was steadily away from the firm Toryism of its founder to the Liberal and Labour camps where now its strength unquestionably lies.

Does this impose especial responsibilities on the Methodism of the present age? Can it be said that any part of her unfulfilled mission is directly concerned with changing the social order?

We live happily in an age when almost every branch of the Holy Catholic Church is sensitive to social problems and not merely sensitive to a few social sins. Methodism has always been to the fore in fighting the classic aversions of the Puritan conscience: intemperance, gambling, and the desecration of Sunday. She has shared also her fellow-Christians' concern over the orphaned and unwanted children, and stretched out willing hands to succour the poor.

All this she has done.

But passing time has posed other and harder problems. It is not as easy as it was to stand where our fathers did concerning Sunday, for instance. The first Lord Stamp was a convinced Methodist, but as Chairman and President of the London, Midland and Scottish Railway he was one of the greatest popularizers of Sunday travel. Mr. J. Arthur Rank is a Methodist by birth and by conviction, yet his Herculean efforts to improve British films has made him one of the main supporters of the Sunday cinema. Let the eager critic pause a moment and put himself in their place.

Yet these personal perplexities are small in comparison with the harder problems which press.

It is not what we have called social salvage work which has been neglected, nor yet those special concerns of the Puritan conscience which we have set down. The great need is for large Christian sociological thinking and exposition—the communal outworking of our doctrine of holiness which Dale said we lacked 'the genius or the courage' to see through.

Odd as it would sound to our spiritual forebears, we are compelled to say that personal piety is not enough. Though on one definition of the word it can be said that sin belongs only to persons and cannot inhere in a 'system', yet a deeper scrutiny of modern life shows that it does attach to systems and that, in many spheres, man's 'sin' becomes involuntary. To teach men to be conscientious in a society which turns their good to evil—as when we burned the wheat on which no profit could be made—is to tread the borders of social insanity.

How to get God's order on the earth!—there is the problem. And it isn't a problem only of a feeble will. It has to be thought out before it can be wrought out. Many Christians—many Methodists—haven't *seen* it yet. Religion, they think, is individual goodness. Wrestling with social and political theories, even though it be undertaken in the Name and to the glory of God, seems hardly a spiritual occupation to them. So far from seeing that religion and politics belong at a deep level together, they dread the contact lest it contaminate the things of God.

So far as my observation goes, these timid souls belong to two classes. Some of them are simple, unreflective Christians whose religion is real even though it may be narrow and who are just 'not bothered' by the problems of communal life. Jesus satisfies them. They meditate on Him, and their meditation is sweet. They ask no more of life—humble though their circumstances be—than quietly to 'walk with God to heaven'.

The others are often people of privilege who—I say it tenderly—are (unconsciously, perhaps) on the defensive concerning their privileges. 'What need is there of radical social change?' they inquire. 'All we want in industry, for instance, is the "team spirit". Goodwill would change everything. Love is the key.'

How true it all is—and yet how inadequate. Goodwill is no substitute for social justice and no cure for incomplete or muddled thinking. Charity and social paternalism will always have their place, one supposes, in this world, but neither can be ultimately accepted in place of a man's rights.

Want of thought and want of heart are both involved in this. God's will must be done in the community as well as in our private lives. The demand for social change grows in volume. Some who are most strident in their call for it are most scornful of religion.

They do not see the world as God's. The idea of 'a family in Him' is parsonic patter. Christianity, they sometimes grotesquely suggest, has been nothing but a device to keep the poor in their place.

> *The rich man in his castle,*
> *The poor man at his gate,*
> *God made them, high or lowly,*
> *And order'd their estate.*

Who—that is in touch with working men outside the Churches—but has heard them chant that verse with mock solemnity—and then spit!

How can we win the labouring classes back again to respect and love and adoration of our Lord—and how can we win them also to belief in the mission of the Church?

Time was, as we have shown, when Methodism had an unusually firm grip on the working classes. Her ministry was—and is—largely recruited from its ranks. The way to the university for those who got there was usually the way of midnight oil, scholarships, and furtive saving.

There are great gains in this. The Church of England used to be called 'the Tory party at prayer'. This was never wholly true. The Church of F. Denison Maurice, of Charles Kingsley, of Thomas Hughes, of Scott Holland, and supremely of William Temple, was far from dead to social problems.

Yet there was enough truth in the gibe to give it currency, for nobody missed the point.

I believe that one of the richest contributions the Free Churches—and Methodism among them—have made to the life of England has been the plain proof that Christianity need not be reactionary or opposed to the passion for social reform.

One glance at the history of Europe in the past generation makes the point clear.

In Russia, Christianity became identified with superstition and the oppression of the people, not because the ordinary priest was himself an oppressor, but because he normally made no protest and drugged the people into acquiescence. When—in their hour of opportunity—the people rose to rend their tyrannical overlords, their fury flamed out to the Church as well. Vital religion might have been saved in Russia by a strong evangelical Nonconformity.

How has it been in those countries on the Continent where the Roman Catholic Church has held a dominating position? Until comparatively recent times, to be a liberal or a social reformer was almost inevitably to be anti-Church and usually an unbeliever altogether. When men only see the Church linked up with political reaction it is inevitable that they should conclude that the Faith itself is out of harmony with social righteousness and freedom of thought.

That might have happened in England. Free Churchmen—and Methodists among them—have had their conspicuous part in preventing it through two centuries. E. A. Payne says: 'It is not fanciful to connect the failure of political democracy on the Continent with the absence there of a sturdy religious tradition of the Free Church type'[1].

The mass of people in England may be quite unaware of this debt, and there may still be certain ecclesiastics who regard the Free Churches as little more than 'vulgar fractions', but in the new age already dawning the relation of the Gospel and social progress will need to be shown more urgently than ever. The working classes are going to take an increasing share in local and national government. Their firm attachment to the faith would mean much for the future of England. Any branch of the Church that has the ear of the common people has, therefore, a special responsibility in this age.

Perhaps I may be forgiven the suspicion of vanity if I set down the tribute paid to the Methodist ministry by that distinguished litterateur and scholar, the late Dr. Edward Thompson, Fellow of Oriel College, Oxford. He says of our ministry:

It draws from every social stratum except the highest and next to the highest, and builds up from them the finest brotherhood of service in the world. It knows the people. Not the people who enter

[1] *The Free Church Tradition in the Life of England*, p. 151.

Parliament or govern the Empire or write the books that get read and praised. *But the people.*[1]

Not claiming for a moment any monopoly of this knowledge, let us speak to the people the whole counsel of God. Let us declare that by His grace and guidance alone can the social order be worthily changed.

CHAPTER FIVE

IN BEING A BRIDGE-CHURCH

Few christians can be found today who are ready to defend the disunion of the Church on the ground that it is a good thing. The overwhelming majority of believers regard it as a calamity and one of the reasons why the world has the Faith in derision.

The degree of distress, however, that this disunion causes varies a great deal. Some Christians believe that it is easily possible to exaggerate the seriousness of 'our unhappy divisions'. After all, they argue, God knows His own. The members of His Church (clearly cherished by Him) are in all Communions, and some of them, conceivably, in none, so that our reckonings of membership as it is understood in heaven must be rough in any case. Nor is unity as such any guarantee of spiritual power. Vastness in a Church as in a business brings losses as well as gains. The larger a Church becomes the more remote and impersonal its direction must be.

Unfortunate as our divisions are, these Christians say, it is simply a consequence of human diversity and merely illustrates again that we look at things in different ways.

[1] *John Arnison*, p. 293 (my italics).

C

It will cease to seem important, they remind us, the moment we are joined to the Church above.

But this is cold comfort to those who regard schism as a sin; who are utterly downcast at the thought of denominational divisions; who plead early and late with the Saviour that His dismembered Body may be made whole again.

The wide earth cries out, they feel, for the unity of Christendom. Our poor bewildered race, dwelling in atomic night, will never listen to the Churches, but might listen to the Church. How can we help humanity to forgo the follies of national sovereignty and fuse into a Parliament of Man if we cannot transcend our own denominational loyalties in love of the *one* Holy Catholic Church? Well might the statesmen of the world meet any confident ecclesiastic coming forward with a formula for world unity with the sharp admonition of our Lord: 'Physician, heal thyself.'

Nor is this the only reason which impels us toward unity. The fearful inefficiency in Church work which disunion fosters is known to all. Some areas are over-churched and others sadly neglected. Man-power is misapplied. When one sees two churches standing cheek by jowl in some thinly populated area, it is hard to believe that there was ever need for both and one is left with the inference that it was denominational pride rather than the zeal of the Lord which put them up.

The situation on the Mission Field is, in some ways, sadder still. It is true that the chief Protestant Churches now respect each other's spheres of service, avoid competition, and work together in schools and hospitals, but even then there is some inevitable carry-over of ancient ecclesiastical controversies, and the steps of native peoples coming out of darkness into light have been impeded by the stones which wall one Western Communion from another. One thinks of Mtesa, the paramount chief of Uganda (of whom H. M. Stanley wrote so warmly), evangelized first by German missionaries, then by Anglicans, and then all confused again by French Roman Catholics, putting his poor head in his hands and saying in despair: 'Has every nation of white men a different religion?'[1]

Add to all this the incontrovertible fact that the New Testament has no counsel of conduct for one denomination in regard to another because the unity of the Church is assumed in the Book of God, and add also the distress of conscience which every sensitive Christian feels in the presence of his Lord when he remembers that there are barriers between him and other disciples, and the cause of reunion can never be one of tepid interest or mild concern.

God wills union. The unity of the Church is dear to His heart. The way thither may be long and circuitous and I shall know the rapture of it only in glory.

But never let me deny the obligation to seek it assiduously, nor ever cease to pray for the peace of Jerusalem. If the facts of the situation quite resolutely forbid a swift solution, let me at least keep my eye fixed on the distant target nor fail in those special responsibilities which every follower of John Wesley must surely feel.

For the Founder of Methodism was a man of truly Catholic spirit. He had all that Calvin and Luther had to give him in one hand, and another hand free to take the rich treasures of Catholic spirituality. The thought of schism was abhorrent to him. If the need of the unchurched masses and the spiritual insensitivity of his ecclesiastical superiors forced him into actions which were bound to issue in division, he hoped and prayed that the division would be avoided.

[1] C. D. Michael, *James Hannington*, p. 75.

His plea for love and co-operation in Christian service, despite opposed views of Church order and differences in Biblical interpretation, is known far beyond the borders of Methodism.

> I do not mean, 'Embrace my modes of worship'; or, 'I will embrace yours'. This also is a thing which does not depend either on your choice or mine. We must both act as each is fully persuaded in his own mind. Hold you fast that which you believe is most acceptable to God, and I will do the same. I believe the Episcopal form of church government to be scriptural and aposto-lical. If you think the Presbyterian or Independent is better, think so still, and act accordingly. I believe infants ought to be baptized; and that this may be done either by dipping or sprinkling. If you are otherwise persuaded, be so still, and follow your own persuasion. It appears to me, that forms of prayer are of excellent use, particularly in the great congregation. If you judge extemporary prayer to be of more use, act suit-ably to your own judgement. My sentiment is, that I ought not to forbid water, wherein persons may be baptized; and that I ought to eat bread and drink wine, as a memorial of my dying Master: however, if you are not convinced of this, act according to the light you have. I have no desire to dispute with you one moment upon any of the preceding heads. Let all these smaller points stand aside. Let them never come into sight. 'If thine heart is as my heart,' if thou lovest God and all mankind, I ask no more: 'give me thine hand.'[1]

There are, moreover, other reasons even more pertinent than loyalty to John Wesley which makes the witness of the modern Methodist important in the present-day religious life of England.

[1] E. H. Sugden, *The Standard Sermons of John Wesley*, Vol. II, p. 139.

Methodism, as we have seen (pp. 16f), is a 'bridge-Church'. She stands between the Established and the Free Churches with affection and indebtedness in her heart to both. She has a task of interpretation both ways. The familiar distinction of Troeltsch between the 'sect type' and the 'Church type' is too rigid to comprehend Methodism. Both in its origin as a society within the Church of England and in its development as a branch of the Holy Catholic Church (exceeding in size the Anglican Church from which it sprang), Methodism has administered the Word and Sacraments to a world community and fits with neatness into neither of Troeltsch's types if one implies the exclusion of the other. Set forms of prayer are not a recent development among the followers of John Wesley, nor merely a part of the general groping in the Free Churches for a more ordered worship, but belong to the oldest and most established traditions of this people. A bishop is no figure of fear to a typical Methodist. Far the larger part of World Methodism has always been episcopally led.

Nor has the local Methodist church ever been 'independent' in the sense that a Congregational or Baptist church is independent: free, that is, to appoint whom it will as a minister and enjoying complete autonomy. The highly organized life of the circuit, district, and whole Connexion makes it fairly simple for a Methodist to understand parochial and diocesan life, while his democratic privileges in synod and annual conference, and his right to appoint his own leaders, gives precious meaning to the description of Methodism as a *Free* Church. The idea of their Moderators or Presidents being chosen by Prime Ministers is repugnant to all Free Churchmen. The Crown Rights of the Redeemer are dear to them. The Church, they hold, has received from Him alone 'the right and power, subject to no civil authority, to legislate and to adjudicate finally in all matters of doctrine, worship, government, and discipline in the Church'.

Here, then, is a task still to be done. In the movement toward organic union of the Church in England, let Methodism build her bridge here: let her leaders and people—in no way magnifying their own importance—humbly accept at God's hand this ministry of interpretation as between the Church of England on the one hand and the Free Churches on the other, and pray that at the last their roadmaking may not be found altogether unworthy as a highway for the King.

But let the work proceed with patient understanding of the difficulties which bar the way.

It sometimes happens that in their zeal for swift success the earnest advocates of reunion misinterpret the motives of those who hesitate, depreciate their own Communion and hinder the cause they have most at heart.

One Methodist writer lays it down that 'boldly and dogmatically to insist that Methodism's task is not yet done is to mistake dogma for truth and makes its appeal only to incorrigible sectarians. It is clap-trap that serves as an altogether unworthy substitute for moral insight'.[1]

The God-given longing for reunion does not require that a man become scornful of, or indifferent to, his denominational distinctiveness. The two loyalties can live together. The contradiction is superficial and the synthesis deep.

When the passion to 'get together' leads people to jettison things for which their fathers died and which they themselves hold lightly only because they do not know in experience a Church or a world in which those things are lost, the cause of true religion is harmed. The

[1] *The Kingsway Messenger*, June–July 1946, p. 1.

cost and preciousness of democracy was lost on some people until they had a taste of totalitarianism.

True Catholicism is a *rich* thing. The way to achieve it is not by entering into an unholy barter ('If you give up that, I'll give up this . . .') but rather for each to bring what each has found precious and put it in the common store. It may be that the natural supposition that parts of such a whole will be mutually contradictory, and that 'if you have this you can't have that' will not always prove to be true. Truth is many-faceted. In the history of human thought it has been found repeatedly that controversialists have been right in what they affirmed and wrong only when they denied. I believe that the Spirit of God calls us to a dual task: to work for the true unity of the Body of God and to be unshakenly firm in what we have seen of truth.

Consequently, I do not find it easy to be patient with the constant denigration of their own people uttered by some advocates of early reunion. They are too Christian to criticize other Churches, so they criticize their own. Most Communions are familiar with the type. The wounding things I have heard some Anglo-Catholics utter of the Church of England, and their scathing comments on certain bishops (whom they profess to reverence as their fathers in God), would be funny if they were not profane.

And then, by contrast, these disgruntled people usually speak with extravagant praise of some other Communion toward which their hopes of reunion are plainly set as though the achievement of that degree of ecclesiastical fusion would bring in the Kingdom of God overnight.

The commonest complaint of these malcontents in Methodism is that they can see 'no future' in their branch of the Church.

I have often wondered quite what they meant by that.

I am sure they didn't mean that God had lost interest in, or love for, the followers of John Wesley. Unless their thinking was incredibly shallow, they couldn't mean that a world community numbering many million souls, and—taking the world over—steadily increasing in numbers, was in process of rapid decay and doomed to swift extinction.

They can only mean, I suppose, that when they look forward into ages unborn they see 'no future' for Methodism as a separate Communion distinct from other branches of the Church and continuing just in the way she has travelled in the two hundred years which lie behind.

But if that is what they mean, the same thing can be asserted of every other Communion as well. When I look beyond the immediate future, I cannot see the Baptist Church—though it is a world-wide Communion—dwelling in separation for ever and ever.

Nor yet the Church of England.

Nor yet the Church of Rome.

God has purposes and plans for His people which encompass them all in the unity of His embracing love, and to say that one can see no future for Methodism is either (according to the thought in a man's mind) to utter a platitude or confess to a strange blindness. God does not call a Communion into being and make a people of those who were no people, and beget saints among them, in order to cast them off. The test of 'fruits' will still stand. God is in any Church which can grow saints.

Not even the enemies of Methodism—if such there be—will deny that this Communion has its thousands of obscure saints.

Moreover, those earnest advocates of swift organic union, who seem to discover all the opponents to their plans in their own Communion, must be on their guard against impugning the motives of other men. It really is not enough to give a bright exhortation to the Churches to 'get together'. Every little while an earnest Christian utters such an exhortation, sometimes in manifest love and sometimes in an impatient and hectoring manner, utterly bewildered that the whole of Christendom isn't united already. He is seldom a serious theologian, either does not know the difficulties which impede the way or makes light of things dear to other people, and is aggrieved when somebody points out that, if the things which divide Christians are few in comparison with those which unite them, they are far from being negligible neverthe-less.

As I see it, much as I long that it might be, there is no further act of organic reunion practicable for Methodists in this generation. If one were to assert that the way is barred by the strongly held convictions of other Christians, that is, of course, only another way of saying that the way is barred by one's own convictions too. The thing is inevitably two-sided like a sheet of paper or a medal or a coin.

To assert that another Christian's belief in Apostolical Succession (for instance) is a barrier to union is only another way of asserting that one's own *disbelief* in Apostolical Succession is a barrier to union. If we could all conscientiously think alike, the completest reunion would be possible in the shortest time—on the lines laid down by Pope Pius the Eleventh in 1928 when he said: 'There is but one way in which the unity of Christians may be fostered and that is by furthering the return to the one true Church of Christ . . .' i.e. the Roman Catholic Church.

But when men differ about what is true and differ so deeply that they would cheerfully die for the difference, there is little more to be said about organic reunion.

Federation can be discussed and plans considered for still closer co-operative working even while the articles of faith remain unidentical. Love and understanding can be fostered so that there is no failure in brotherliness—and hence no temptation to persecution. Reunion can be clearly recognized as the ultimate divine purpose, but when all the facts have been honestly surveyed and un-bridgeable difficulties laid bare, there is need for holy acquiescence in differences irreconcilable as yet.

It is not supine indifference to a tragic situation. The man who speaks with heat about the sin and costliness of disunity, and charges his fellow-Christians with blindness to the tragedy of the situation, is overstating his case. Some of the men who have spent the longest time in seeking the path to reunion are among those most sure that it does not belong to practical church politics at the present time. Bishop Hensley Henson expressed the experience of others who have served on reunion committees (and who are not cynics) when he remarked on 'the interminable discussions . . . which ever traverse the same cycle, and conclude in the same fiasco'.[1]

For the Methodist (in his bridge position between the Anglican and Free Churches), the Anglo-Catholic bars the approach one way. No service of Holy Communion among the Methodists is a true sacrament, as the Anglo-Catholic understands it, not only because Methodist ministers are not real ministers of the Church of God but because the sacrament is taken with unfermented wine! The Anglo-Catholic Bishop of the Windward Islands returned from his distant diocese to preside over the Annual Meeting of the Church Union in 1946. The meeting was held in a Methodist Hall. He said that 'the people of England must stand up for their rights and privileges. There was the question of reunion with

[1] *Retrospect of an Unimportant Life*, Vol. II, p. 370.

Protestant Sectarians'. All Church people 'must stand up as one man and resist' it.[1]

It is a mark of Christian grace to respect the sincerely held opinions of other Christians, but does any honest student of the contemporary religious situation think that organic reunion is round the corner?

The Archbishop of Canterbury has finely and frankly inquired of the Free Churches whether or not they desire reunion but knowing the opposition to reunion among the Anglo-Catholics, might not the Free Churchman ask himself whether the Anglicans are ready to risk rending their Church on this issue? Is it not probable that they will counsel waiting and talk of the efficacy of 'time'?

Or, if the Methodist turns the other way, and seeks organic union with the Free Churches, he meets a conscientious and obdurate impediment among the Baptists.

Let us speak of it with profound respect. Many of our Baptist friends hold that the New Testament lays it down that Church membership and the Holy Communion are only for those who have received believer's baptism. They say, affectionately but frankly, that they cannot compromise there. It is the *Master's* rule: not theirs.

Out of respect for these iron convictions, conscientiously held by some of their constituent Churches, the Baptist Union has declared that organic reunion (even with other Free Churches) is a matter they cannot usefully discuss.

Perhaps these facts will convince eager Methodists, disposed to say that the chief barrier to Church unity is the sluggishness of their own Communion, that there are other barriers also, more deeply set and theologically based. Perhaps they will concede as well that there are solid reasons for asserting that another big step in organic reunion is clearly not possible for Methodists at present. It

[1] *The Guardian*, 26th July 1946.

will temper their disappointment to remember that their own union of 1932 is far from being fully consummated, and there is much work still to do in many parts of the country before our people are one in heart and soul.

Ecclesiastical machinery is heavy and slow moving. The union of Churches in Canada was under discussion for thirty-one years. Even so, the Anglican Church was not included, nor yet the Baptists, and a large section of the Presbyterians contracted out. In Scotland, the union of 1929 was debated for twenty years. The first committee appointed to collect information for Methodist Union in England received its instructions in 1913, and the union was enacted in 1932. Nearly twenty years, and not a serious theological difference in debate!

Nor can it be denied that when a Church is preoccupied with the kind of discussion on polity and theology which organic union involves there is inevitably some direction of effort away from evangelism and the building up of the Church.

It ought not to be so. In our future efforts toward unity we must vow that it will *not* be so.

But it *has* been in time past!

Assume the role of an optimist for a moment and suppose that serious discussions for the reunion of the Anglican and Free Churches in England began at once. Assume also that they moved as 'swiftly' in England as in South India. The consummation which is so devoutly to be wished would be achieved by 1973.

It is still a thing to work for, but it is most definitely work for posterity. If it depresses a man to feel that he is no nearer to it than that, let him comfort himself with the assurance that even in these days of sad division he can still offer Christ to all about him and none can prevent him doing the work of an evangelist.

Evangelism does not wait on Church union. Because it is probable that evangelism would be assisted by such union, some of the advocates of amalgamation are speaking as though it is a *necessary* pre-requisite of winning men to Christ.

That is not so.

It is one of the sad curiosities of ecclesiastical history that great tides of genuine evangelism have been the *cause* of division: not usually by the will of the inspired leaders but because the new wine has burst the old bottles.

Is it melancholy to conclude that we have not reached the stage for serious discussion of further organic reunion? It *can* be discussed, of course, but the discussion will be largely academic. If the way to corporate union is the way, first, of courteous and affectionate understanding; secondly, of active co-operation in Christian service (with occasional acts of worship); and, finally, of organic unity (probably by way of federation first), then we are definitely in the second stage so far as the non-Roman Communions in England are concerned at present. The work of the British Council of Churches and the Free Church Federal Council is work at our point of need. It draws us into fellowship not chiefly for discussion but to *do* something to extend God's kingdom. Our fellowship is a by-product of service. The ache to 'belong' to one another grows with mutual knowledge, and the day will come when it will be widely felt that we cannot live apart.

It may be that our best policy in this age—as, indeed, the Archbishop of Canterbury suggested in his sermon before the University of Cambridge on 4th November 1946—is to set aside the hope of organic union at present and not toy with the thought of federation either (because federation does not restore the 'free circulation of the life of Christ between the folds of His flock') but to aim rather at full communion with one another even while 'the folds remain distinct'.[1]

Conversations are proceeding with that in mind and Methodists are taking an eager part in them but the more urgent tasks are not at headquarters. The lead from 'above' must be matched with desire from 'below'. Any resolute Christian with a will to this can begin to play his part in his own locality. He can be a bridge-builder there—and if he be a follower of John Wesley he will recognize a special obligation to build a bridge between the Church from which John Wesley came and the Church God used John Wesley unwillingly to found.

Considerable progress has already been made. Neither liturgy, episcopacy, nor establishment are quite the controversial subjects that they were. Many Free Churchmen are using liturgies and see no insuperable objection to episcopacy as a form of Church government. On the other hand, there are many in the Anglican Church who are experimenting with non-liturgical worship, are seeking a constitutional episcopacy, and would prefer establishment on the Scottish model to the all but indefensible form of it which they have now.

Apostolical Succession remains the hard dividing line still, and here—from the time of John Wesley—Methodism has been in firm opposition. Her 'bridge' cannot span this gulf.

Yet the work of mutual understanding which will lead to unity still needs to be done and no achievement of unity becomes clear to the plain man until it becomes local. Let the work for it be local too! In simple acts of Christian neighbourliness let us stretch out willing hands in our own localities to all who love our Lord. Let us be patient with misunderstanding, meek before the accusations of

[1] *Cambridge Review*, 9th November 1946, p. 118.

those who would unchurch us altogether, invincible in hope, and, manifestly, 'the friends of all and the enemies of none'.

CHAPTER SIX

IN REDEEMING RURAL AREAS

THERE ARE, in round figures, about 11,000 rural parishes belonging to the Established Church in England, and about 7,000 Methodist chapels in the same areas. If we add to this last number the many hundreds of places of worship belonging to the other Free Churches, we get the normal pattern of our rural religious life. The strength of the Roman Catholic Church in this country is not, generally speaking, in the villages, and no other form of faith has any firm grip on agricultural areas at all. In thousands of villages in this country the opportunity of worship is offered in the Established and the Free Church, and the Free Church, in far the larger number of these rural communities, is the Methodist chapel. No one who motors through our green and pleasant land can miss these little bethels, for they are nearly as familiar as the parish church and the village inn.

Their architecture has often been the subject of caustic comment. Some of them, it is true, have a simple dignity of their own and fit with modest naturalness into the countryside, but the majority of them have no comeliness and hundreds are all but hideous. Only the most resolute religious conviction, one feels, could have led people away from the beauty and the holy past of the parish church and made them worship in these barn-like structures where nothing but the glory of the true

Shekinah could have hid their ugliness from the worshippers' eyes.

Every little while some public comment is made upon the aesthetic offensiveness of the village chapel. Hugh Massingham and Sidney Dark were at it a year or two ago.[1] Without endeavouring to deny the substance of the charge, one feels provoked by its repetition to point out another aspect of the matter.

Who built these village chapels? Who covered the countryside with these 'repulsive' structures?

They were built, for the most part, by the pence of farm labourers. They were reared to the glory of God by men who were earning seven, eight, or ten shillings a week as agricultural workers and bringing up large families, and who tithed themselves and gave of their penury that they might worship in their own way.

Many of these chapels were put up in the second quarter of the nineteenth century when the Church of England was building the 'Waterloo churches' paid for by £1,500,000 of public money.[2] The 'Waterloo churches' are not generally regarded as artistic triumphs, but, even so, it isn't hard to build right up to the aesthetic standards of the day when somebody else is paying for it.

These are things one knows but never mentions until repeated gibes at the 'bastard gothic' of Nonconformists and savage comments on her 'ugly bethels' provoke a frank word of rejoinder. Our glorious parish churches are dear to Free Churchmen. There are senses

---

[1] *New Statesman and Nation*, 7th April 1945, p. 222; cf. *Spectator*, 6th September 1946, p. 232.

[2] Parliament voted £1,000,000 in 1818 and about another £500,000 in 1824. Lord Liverpool frankly stated that the grant was made ' to remove Dissent' (*Parliamentary Debates*, xxxviii, p. 710). Lord Holland, in the same debate, characterized the attitude to Dissenters thus: ' You gentlemen, who pay for yourselves, who pay for your own chapels and your own clergy, in addition to paying tithes to ours, shall also contribute to the erection of those churches in which you have no interest whatever' (ibid., pp. 716f).

in which they are ours as well as our Church of England neighbours. Our distant forbears shared in their building and drenched the place with their prayers.

I go occasionally to a lovely village in a corner of Essex and stand by the headstones of my own ancestors. As I gaze on seven hundred years of history in the noble parish church I cannot deny the aching desire which fills my heart to 'belong' to it again; to take the Communion where my forbears took it; to have my own place where they had theirs; to see the Church of England the Church of the English people once more.

But there is no private way back. Religion became real to me among the people called Methodists. The stain of sin, the wonder of forgiveness, the rapture of religion, the way to an intimate and personal experience of God,

> *The speechless awe that dares not move*
> *And all the silent heaven of love,*

it all came to me in spite of the sticky varnish on the pitch-pine pews and Victorian stencilling upon the walls. The clouds unfolded—and I knew! To others, no doubt, in other ways. But thus to me! In my heart I said: 'This people shall be my people and their God my God.'

And thus it has been during more than two centuries of this changeful, mortal life for tens of thousands in the villages of England.

If I might seem to speak with undue bias toward the country chapel, let me call as witness one who was long a country rector himself and is now the Master of the Temple, Canon Harold Anson. He says:

I want to say how deeply I have been struck in many places I have lived in, by the piety, self-denial, and courage of those who maintain, without endowments or social prestige, the village chapel. Nothing short of a profound sense of religion could give people the enthusiasm which lies behind these little centres of Christian fellowship. For years together the parish church may be practically dead. The chapel salvages those whose lives would otherwise be wrecked. They attach themselves to the chapel and enjoy its fellowship. Then, after many years, the moribund parish church revives: a new parson, full of energy, rounds up his wandering flock, perhaps preaching, not too charitably, on the sin of schism; and the chapel is reduced once more to its original numbers. Over and over again I have admired the zeal of these chapel folk, and envied their mutual love.

No Church will ever be the Church of the English people which does not include these valiant communities. No Church can afford to despise these people who, with no rich people and no ancient endowments to support them, maintain their own cause unaided, and are, generally speaking, forward in every public need.[1]

It is not surprising, therefore, in the light of so gracious a tribute to the village chapel, that Methodism should watch her rural work with tender concern and appoint periodic commissions to report on its condition.

At times the fears for the work have been foolish and alarmist, and the impression has gone abroad that, in comparison with the towns, the Methodism of the villages was in rapid decay. Things can be bad without being as bad as that, and the towns have too many problems of their own to feel superior.

. The fact is that some of the finest Methodism still to be found is in village communities. It may be that the pull of counter-attractions is felt less in rural areas than in urban districts, and although the bus and the motor-

[1] Harold Anson, *Looking Forward*, p. 239.

cycle offer quick transport to the cinema, the village chapel still has a better chance to be the social as well as the spiritual centre of community life than the chapel in the town.

If, moreover, the revival of agriculture is continued and there is a return to the soil, the backward drift of village Methodism may be arrested and a new era of spiritual service begin.

Because—let there be no doubt about it—the redemption of rural areas is an urgent task calling for all the resources of the whole Church of God. Townsmen often have sentimentalized pictures of the country. Their use of the threadbare phrase 'God made the country but man made the towns' illustrates it. Only ignorance could suppose that the beauty of the country with its chequer-board of well-tilled fields, and groomed hedges, and cleaned-out ditches, owed next to nothing to the skilled husbandry of man. Left to herself, nature would riot even in England, and most of the beauty the week-ender admires would vanish in a year of neglect.

But the townsman's sentimentalism doesn't end there.

He often speaks as though sin is a monopoly of cities: that, because it is easier in some ways to feel nearer God in rural England, so it is easier in the country to live the holy life.

I doubt if it makes a ha'p'orth of difference to the quest for holiness whether or not you live in the country: it all turns on whether or not you live in God.

Sin is rampant in rural areas as well as in the slums. The bawdy story goes the round. Animosities are felt and sometimes fostered into flaming feuds which can last among country people for years. Pre-marital and extra-marital sex relationships are not uncommon. The village often has its prostitute, not handling half a dozen men per night, maybe, like her sister in the city, but plying the same shameful trade and needing the same tender Saviour.

God's people in the countryside are as much in the battle for righteousness as those in the towns. The numbers engaged in the contest are smaller, but the fight is the same. How glorious it is when their sense of mutual dependence and kinship in Christ enables them to transcend all their denominational differences and battle together for God.

I go now and then to a village where—as in thousands of others—the community is served both by the parish church and the Methodist chapel. The relationship between the two in this particular village is beautiful indeed. The vicar is a father in God to all the people, and when the Methodist minister comes out from the neighbouring town he is welcomed as a brother by all. The members of the Women's Bright Hour and the Mother's Union are sisters together. The Methodist Guild is the guild of the whole village. The religious services of church and chapel are announced on the same bill. Everybody in the place seems to speak about 'our' church and 'our' chapel.

I suppose that a certain kind of ecclesiastic would be distressed by all this. If he wouldn't call it 'wrong', he might call it 'irregular'.

But it is very beautiful, none the less, and the fight for righteousness goes well in that village. Our God is marching on!

Alas! As I go about this England I meet a contrary situation, too. I come to places where clergymen of Anglo-Catholic convictions seem to miss no opportunity of stressing the invalid 'orders' of their Free Church brethren, oppose any suggestion of co-operation 'on principle', and make life desperately hard for little children in the village school because they attend chapel on Sundays. In some rural areas our people are publicly snubbed.

Fortunately this is not common, but then, on the other hand, it is not really rare. Most ministers who have 'travelled' ten or fifteen years have had some personal experience of it.

In a large city the problem is not acute. People can easily find the 'brand' of churchmanship they want. But what of people in a village similarly encumbered? If the chapel wasn't there what would happen in those places where, as Canon Anson says, the parish church is 'moribund' for years, or where, far from being moribund, it is ministered to by a High Church zealot who wants to deal with his Free Church fellow-Christians as the Roman Church deals with him?

Nor is this situation adequately met on the lines employed by the Vicar of Milton-under-Wychwood in his parish magazine of December 1944, or by the Rector of Westcote in his pamphlet, *Charles Wesley at Westcote*, published in the same year.

These are overt appeals to the local village Methodists to forsake their Methodism and come over in a body to the parish church. One wants to give men of this type full credit for any kindly intentions which lie behind their proselytizing, though it is truly amazing that men are ready to venture into print on such subjects with so slight a knowledge of the people they are addressing.

The Rector of Westcote twelve years after Methodist Union seeks to loosen the loyalty of the local Methodists by saying: '*Wesleyan* ministers are laymen still and have no orders that we can recognize.'[1] He goes on to say that when Pope Leo the Thirteenth said the same thing about Anglican orders he was quite wrong!

There is no way forward on this road. The question of

[1] J. A. Thomas, *Charles Wesley at Westcote*, p. 12.

reunion must be dealt with at a higher level than this. Methodists have the matter much upon their heart, as we have shown, and are ready and eager to discuss it in the full equality of brethren, but, in the meanwhile, is it not plain that we have a task still to do in the villages of our land and the cause of evangelical religion would suffer if we neglected it?

The cure of the ills which afflict our work in the villages begins, I suppose, like so much else in the life of the church, within the soul of the minister.

Even devout men can slip half-unconsciously into regarding their work in the ministry as a 'career' and think, if they do not talk, of 'good' and 'poor' circuits. Country circuits have a way of falling within the second category. The allowances are usually the lowest our Church permits a circuit to pay. The manse is often poorly furnished and ill-cared for. The chances are that it has no telephone—and a man may lose valuable hours running on errands which could be dealt with in moments by phone. The difficulty of covering his wide area often poses the awkward choice between a physical strain with a bicycle or a financial strain with a car.

The idea seems to have spread in some quarters that our rural work is less important, or makes less demands, or is the natural sphere of less able men, and ministers have even been known to shrink from this work, not because they disliked it, or believed it less important themselves, but because *other people* seemed to think so and rather pitied them for being there.

I wish we could recover a new respect for ordinary circuit work and especially for ordinary circuit work in rural areas. It is an unspeakable privilege of which we are altogether unworthy that we should be ministers of the grace of God at all, but the privilege does not vary one iota if we are called to serve our people in the largest centres of population or in the loneliest areas of the fell-side.

Are we not all brethren? Is there not an intimacy and a love among us which has made many marvel? Do we not follow each other around so that the spheres of service in which we move may be exchanged in as little as five years, and does not the family life of our Church mean that the triumph and the problems of every part belong to all?

'The unity of the Church' is a phrase much beloved in some ecclesiastical circles, but in the *practice* of unity Methodism need not be ashamed of her record. The principle of the strong helping the weak is knit into the Methodist system. It finds many expressions. The work of missions abroad, for instance, is not (as in some Churches) the hobby of a few enlightened zealots splendidly running an independent society but the work of the Church *per se*.

So with the toil of rural areas. It is all the work of all. None of us finally chooses his own sphere of work. We go where we are sent. Our invitations are all subject to approval. We have promised God and the Church to 'submit ourselves as sons in the Gospel, to those whom the Methodist Church shall appoint to have the rule over us'. To serve our grand people in the villages is so great an honour that some of the most discerning men among us seek the privilege and know a joy and effectiveness in their ministries which often eludes the men in the inner belt of a great town.

It belongs to the ignorant bumptiousness of some townsmen to suppose that the countryman is a dull-witted, bovine creature, and they dismiss the farm-labourer as an unskilled 'clodhopper'.

If they only knew! What varied skill the changing seasons need! What craft of mind and heart the care of beasts and the tillage of the good earth demands!

We must make no such mistakes in the ministry. The emphasis in rural work may be different, but it is not less skilled. The labour of sermon preparation may be less heavy, but what scope for the office of pastor; what need and opportunity for visitation; what warm-hearted meal-time hospitality in those country homes; what opportunities for quiet talks with lonely people on the things of God.

And, above all else, what holy craft the minister must employ in creating lay-leadership.

Those people are mistaken who toy with the idea that success in Methodism means 'one minister for one church'. They are mistaken every way. No other major denomination has made more use of the laity than Methodism. Not for one week could we continue without this consecrated help.

And if a man could forget that patent fact in a town, how could he possibly forget it in the country?

To foster and train and renew lay-leadership is the first claim on a country minister's time. When he has said his prayers and brooded on the Book of God, he turns his mind over to this. When, years after, he has moved on to other spheres of service, the strength and the permanence and the statesmanship of his work will all be tested here: 'What latent capacity did he discover in unlikely men and women? How did he draw it out? What equipment did he give them for their lonely, local tasks? Have they stood?'

I know something of this work from experience, but more by observing my friends. I have seen the hand-picked utterly-in-earnest people ride in from a score of villages for their weekly fellowship, prayer, and training by their minister in the market town. With each one of them, in complete privacy, he began at a deep level: spoke of his own experience of Christ; told of his own longings for more grace; held out the gift of God in Jesus and put no limit to what grace could do; inflamed holy desire within them and set their gaze upon the heights.

So he led them to the deepest consecration; so he drew them into fellowship with others equally in earnest, and equally ready to take responsibility; so, week by week, he met them in the circuit town and gave his best of prayer and preparation and told them all he knew of inner devotion and the technique of soul-winning and the creation of cells of spiritual life.

So he sent them back to their villages, put them to work, secretly advised on their problems, wrapped them around with prayer and glorified God when, by their endeavours, another cell of fellowship was born.

Preachers and class-leaders, Sunday school teachers, workers in women's meetings—have I not seen them coming for their weekly meal and have I not felt the grandeur and the sweep of this rural toil?

It is a coarse test of value in religious work to measure it by numbers. The annual circuit rally with a visiting preacher is not usually the most spiritually significant hour in the year. It is good to be there, of course; fine to sing without absurdity, 'Like a mighty army moves the Church of God'; grand to see all the keen people in the circuit packed into the town chapel and with chairs down the aisles: but if the little weekly meetings for fellowship are vital in the villages—there is the proof of health.

How to maintain those meetings under devoted and skilled lay leadership is the country minister's supreme task, and when he succeeds in that hard and urgent service the angels rejoice in heaven.

The Report of the last Commission on Rural Methodism was said by some to contain 'nothing new'.

Maybe not! Most people with their finger on the pulse of our village work knew the facts and agreed about the remedy. It was not the business of the Commission to say anything new: they aimed to say something true. The true doesn't become the false when it becomes familiar. The findings merit another glance and a firmer application.

It is still a common sight in the villages of our land to see two Methodist chapels close to one another. It is not unusual to learn that neither is well attended and that one little sanctuary could easily contain both congregations. The unevangelized in the village know these facts and must murmur sarcastically beneath their breath: 'See how these Christians love!'

To what splendid use the redundant chapel might be put. Could it be turned into a Christian youth club? Would the other Churches co-operate in making it, in its modest way, a village community centre? Does the hamlet lack a hall, and could the loved building have a further use that way?

People in villages are often slow to part with their money but very generous in service or kind. Their fine independence and hatred of patronage are virtues if one looks at them in the right way, and they would be more likely to cherish a building they had converted by their own skill and improvization to a communal use.

They need a lead.

In town and village alike our people must learn that Christian work is not confined to the various offices of steward which are recognized in Methodism, nor yet to the regular appointments of the Sunday school. Christian work summons men and women into leadership in public life. If folk of Christian conviction decline to come forward in the service of the community, the lead will be taken by others—perhaps with perilous results.

It must be a matter of delight to all who love our Lord and rural England that the amazing spread of the Women's Institute owes so much to the fine lead of

Christian women from all the Churches—even though formal religion is a subject not discussed.

But there are still thousands of villages without a Women's Institute or the prospect of one. Could that redundant chapel find a use there? Could the gulf between the Christian people and the 'outsiders' (which is as sharp in the village as the town) be bridged in that way? The women have often shown the men the road forward. Could they show it again?

We may leave it there. But if anybody of moderate influence in a wholly urban circuit or central mission felt deeply about rural Methodism and wanted to do something both personal and practical, let him persuade his own Quarterly Meeting to 'adopt' a needy country circuit: one not too far distant; one to which the local preachers could go fairly frequently and with which personal friendships could easily be formed.

The loveliest consequences may follow from this. Town can help country and country town. The city has its link with the good earth, and the rural community feels cared for and brothered.

And not the least happy consequence of this mutually helpful relationship is that the city dweller no longer feels separated from village Methodism but can play his own not unimportant part in the glorious service of rural areas.

CHAPTER SEVEN

IN TEACHING THE USE OF MONEY

IT WAS BALZAC who said more than a century ago: 'The final battle for Christianity will be over the money problem: till that is solved there can be no universal application of Christianity.'

Much that Balzac had in mind when he said that is beyond the range of our interest now, but it will put us on guard against the people who suppose that Christianity and money have nothing to do with one another and that money touches nothing that it does not taint.

The Church as a world-wide institution cannot avoid the problems of money. The maintenance of her buildings, the spread of her missions at home and abroad, the training and sustenance of her ministry, all demand money.

Some individual Christians seek to side-step the problems of money by undertaking full-time religious service on 'faith alone': give themselves, for example, to evangelism in England or overseas without any provision for their material welfare, but just trust that 'the Lord will provide'.

They need money just as much as anybody else. It is no depreciation of the noblest of these souls to admit that, as their need is known in Christian circles, their economic burdens are borne not by angels but by plain men and women who are busy doing their bit of the world's work and who give (often out of their poverty) that these others may devote all their time to the direct service of God.

So *money* hasn't been eliminated—and while the life of such servants of God may appear more precarious, it is not necessarily more holy than the life of those who are sustained in modest ways by funds publicly collected and competently checked.

Of all her money problems, perhaps none is more important to the Church than the maintenance of the ministry—if only because it is more than a money problem. It raises questions of *motives* as well.

There are few texts the truth of which the ordinary man is more ready to admit than the assertion in the first Epistle of Timothy that 'the love of money is a root of all kinds of evil'. Not cynicism, but experience of life, has convinced most people that for money some men will do anything, and that the itch for it is in nearly every palm.

Only rare souls overcome the desire for money. It was said of Leigh Hunt that if he saw something yellow on the grass and hastened forward thinking it was a butter-cup, he would have been genuinely disappointed if it turned out to be a sovereign. But Leigh Hunt was an unworldly soul.

'Familiarity breeds contempt' is a rule which admits of few exceptions, but money is one of them. The more men have, the more, it seems, they want. Like some deadly diabetes of the soul, the thirst grows with drinking. No wonder that men have grown suspicious of one another, especially when they claim to undertake disinterested service. So often, alas, the 'noblest' motives have often proved to have little more than the greed for money underneath them.

Nevertheless, however cynical the ordinary man may become about the dominance of the money motive, there are vocations in which he strongly feels that it should have no place. Conceding, as he must do, that ministers of God should be remunerated, he has a deep conviction that if there is a calling where money must not be the motive for engaging in it, this is the calling. In his own inarticulate way he cannot reconcile the preaching of the homeless Galilean with a well-paid job. Secretly admiring as he does any man who has really mastered the itch for money, he looks for that mastery in those who claim to have received a call from God to proclaim the Gospel of the Carpenter.

Money and the ministry, therefore, is a bigger question

than money. 'What is the aim of these men in engaging in this work?' the plain man asks himself. 'They *say* that God has called them to proclaim a divine message . . . but is there any admixture of baser motive as well?'

Nor does the problem of money and the ministry centre only in the natural man's suspicion of a parson's motives. It is made all the more pertinent in the present age by the growing acknowledgement that 'service' should be the mainspring of a good life whether a man is a minister or not. Men dimly feel (however frail they may be themselves) that the greed for personal gain should be transcended by a higher motive, and that life, when properly understood, is the chance to give ourselves without reserve to some fine purpose independent of large monetary returns. They are groping toward the principle: 'From each according to his ability: to each according to his need.' It is being increasingly felt that the accident of birth and the equipment of gifts savours too much of the fortuitous to be a satisfactory basis for a lifetime of advantage: that because no man chooses his parents or deserves his gifts, the only Christian way of life is for all to give their utmost to the Highest and for all to have their needs fairly met. Dr. John Oman held that 'the beam of hypocrisy which perverts all our judgement of ourselves and of others, is the identification of privilege with merit and not with responsibility'.[1] An increasing number of people want to be rid of that beam.

But how?

Is it practicable in this world—as we know it—to demand from each 'according to his ability' if he is to receive only 'according to his need'?

In the judgement of the majority of people, it is not practicable. The ideal stands tantalizingly before us, but unregenerate human nature stands between. The mass of

[1] *Grace and Personality*, p. 196.

men will not work to a maximum for any 'general' good: they want a plain personal gain as well. They want *individual* reward.

It is often said by men in industries which have fixed rates of wages independent of individual output that such a system of remuneration only puts a premium on incompetence and laziness. The spur of personal necessity has to be applied to so many men to get them to do a hard day's work at all.

Theoretically, the joy of creative (and even mechanical) work, together with the just recognition by society of the exercise of a useful gift, should be stimulus enough to labour (even if men had not the highest motive of glorifying God in their daily toil), but frankly it isn't. When a man notices the sloth of others, and notices also in the passing of months that his own honest toil creates no sense of shame in the lazy but only the amused conviction that he himself is a fool—he begins to lose heart. 'That lazy rascal', he feels, 'is living on my back. I am, indeed, the fool he thinks me.'

A deep and radical change in human nature itself is necessary before the principle of service can be applied. The natural man feels that his gifts are *his*. God may not figure in his thought at all. For *his* brains and *his* hard work he expects his *own* return. He expects it normally in money which he can convert according to his own desires into a car, a larger house, a yacht, more leisure, larger legacies for his children—or early retirement and the 'privilege' of doing no work at all. He may acknowledge a certain ideal quality in the principle of each rendering the utmost according to his ability and receiving no more than he needs, but—he is quite sure on the point—it won't work.

Yet ideals, like the shining summit of Mount Everest, demand to be climbed. If this principle *does* express the

will of God, how can we draw nearer to it? If we are not
prepared to postpone it to some remote time when 'every
one will be converted', what can we do in our generation
to prove to incredulous men that it can be done?

We can illustrate it in the ministry of God!

Where better?

We can put our motives beyond suspicion, and we can
prove the 'impossible' by presenting modern society with
a body of men who, with all their variety of gift, offer their
maximum and take no more than their needs; admit the
inequalities of nature but admit no more; prove that man
can, indeed, toil for the glory of God and the general good
and (his simple needs being justly met) ask for no reward
except to serve God still.

Taking the Church as a whole, we offer no such
impressive example as yet.

When the Archbishop of Canterbury was Bishop of
Chester he said at his Diocesan Conference in 1936 that
if he were a dictator he would 'make every living carry the
same stipend. . . . In addition, from a common fund each
incumbent should receive a personal stipend varying
according to his length of service in the ministry . . . and
any special claims which ought to be recognized. Un-
fortunately we are a long way from that.'[1]

The inequalities of stipends in the Church of England
is almost as common a theme in the Press as it is at open-
air meetings. Nor is it discussed only in the denominational journals,[2] where it might be regarded as a domestic
matter, but in our national journals as well.[3] Sometimes
the correspondents (both clerical and lay) deal with the
inadequate incomes, or with the burdensome and old-
fashioned vicarages, or the years and years since the hard-

[1] *The Times*, 27th May 1936.
[2] e.g., *The Guardian*, 26th July–6th September 1946.
[3] e.g., *The Times*, 6th January–10th February 1945; 8th September–19th
September 1949. *The Spectator*, 19th July–30th August 1946.

working cleric had a holiday.[1] Sometimes the vicar's
brave wife writes to admit that never since she wed, 'in
spite of plain living and few holidays', has she 'known
relief from financial anxiety'.[2] The wife of a young
'priest-in-charge' speaks of her difficulties of managing
on £180 a year,[3] and another wife of a clergyman made
ends meet only by sleeping with her children 'in otherwise
empty rooms on a top floor with winter clothes for cover,
so that we could use our furniture and bedding for paying-
guests'.[4]

Similar sad stories come from other sources as well.
Lord Inman tells of a vicar carried into Charing Cross
Hospital in a weak state whose circumstances were so lean
that after the usual deductions from his income had been
made he had fifty-shillings a week left to clothe, feed, and
educate his family.[5] Another cleric, who had been in the
active ministry for thirty-eight years, and whose ability
might be judged by the fact that he was twice nominated
for a canonry, worked out that his income over the entire
period of his ministry was a shade over £210 per annum.[6]
It is on this background that the startling advertisement
must be read: 'Clergyman, tired of money worries, seeks
secular employment: M.A. Oxon., under 40, married,
energetic; any honest livelihood considered, secretarial,
manual, menial. Please any help or offers.'[7]

Not that it must be supposed that there is any whining
in this recurrent correspondence. These are the letters of
brave men and women. None of them appears to have
expected that the ministry would be easy or to be un-
mindful of the fact that many of the people to whom they

[1] *The Guardian*, 2nd August 1946.
[2] idem, 16th August 1946.
[3] idem, 30th August 1946.
[4] idem, 6th September 1946.
[5] *The Times*, 11th November 1945.
[6] *The Spectator*, 30th August 1946.
[7] *Daily Graphic*, 29th July 1946.

ministered were receiving less than they did themselves. If any hint of sharpness appears in their letters it turns on the *inequalities* of things—the lack of elementary justice and the disregard of impartiality. A lay correspondent points out[1] that two of the livings advertised in the same issue of a Church newspaper[2] show so marked a contrast as this: (a) £405 per annum for a parish of 10,955 people, (b) £933 per annum for a parish with 381. The incomes were net in both cases and with a house.

Or if the clergyman looks through the years to the time of retirement the same sharp inequality confronts him. Some write expressing their pain at the unevenness of pensions.[3] A diocesan bishop receives a pension of £800; a suffragan £500; an incumbent, if he has been in the ministry for forty to fifty years and made his annual contribution to the Pensions Board throughout that period, £200.[4]

People are aware of these contrasts. They bring up the subject not infrequently at religious meetings in the open-air. Speakers of all denominations have to meet them. It would be wrong to suggest that it is no business of the questioner. He belongs to the nation and has a right to be interested in the *national* Church. The Church claims to instruct him in holy things. The bishops help to make his laws.

The subject, moreover, is discussed freely in the newspapers. It appears to be useless to tell the people that when the late Dr. Winnington Ingram was Bishop of London and entertained the unemployed dockers to tea in his palace and his guests complained that they were living then on 5d. a day with 2d. a day for each child, the genial bishop took out his own balance

---

[1] *The Guardian*, 27th July 1945.
[2] idem, 13th July 1945.
[3] idem, 6th September 1946.
[4] *The Times*, 18th November 1944; cf. *The Guardian*, 6th September 1946.

sheet and showed them how it ran: *Income*, £10,000 *a year: outgo* £10,600.[1] The dockers didn't know how much it cost to keep a palace. . . !

Keen minds, of course, are being turned to this problem in the Anglican Church. Things are better. They are going, it is hoped, to be better still. Palaces are being turned into Diocesan Houses. *The Times* supplied the details when the late Bishop of Lincoln effected the change. 'The income of the See of Lincoln is £4,500 a year, but under the new scheme the bishop will receive a salary of £2,400 a year, out of which he will have to pay rent and rates (approximately £300 a year) for his new house and £80 a year pension contribution. The Ecclesiastical Commissioners will pay clerical and travelling expenses up to approximately £1,000 a year.'[2]

It will not be assumed, of course, that this problem belongs only to the Established Church. By no means! It is inevitable that where the principle of 'independency' is established, the possibility of these inequalities is established too. The practice also.

Speaking on 'The Economics of Congregationalism'[3] at the London Congregational Union, the Rev. R. Morton Stanley surveyed the minimum stipends paid in Congregational churches in various parts of the country. Ten counties, it seems, 'pay on the lowest scale, £200 to £220 with manses. . . . In one county the minimum for List A is £180 per annum, and in this county (unlike the practice elsewhere) List B men are on the same level. The Home Mission Fund Committee of the Congregational Union suggest a new minimum to be *aimed* at: List A in towns, £275 and manse: country pastorates,

[1] *The Methodist Times and Leader*, 21st February 1935.
[2] 6th June 1945.
[3] *The Christian World*, 29th November 1945.

£225 and manse. List B: towns, £225 and manse: country, £200 and manse '.[1]

But Mr. Stanley deliberately stepped aside from his theme to stress a conviction which his researches had borne in upon him. '*The disparity between the highest and the lowest is far too great.*'

Here, again, then, the principle is not accepted: 'From each according to his ability: to each according to his need.'

In the Baptist Church responsibility for minimum stipends is borne by the Sustentation Fund, together with the new Home Work Fund. This fund was promoted toward the end of 1943 partly because it was felt that the aid given toward the maintenance of the ministers was inadequate. The intention was that, generally speaking, all accredited Baptist Ministers, being married, should receive a minimum salary of £250 a year (estimating the value of a manse at £30 per annum).[2] The Baptist Church is serious in its intention to reach and increase this minimum, and it may confidently be expected to do so for all the churches in the Union which are linked up with the Funds. There are, of course, Baptist churches not associated with the Union, and the minimum rule does not apply to them. There is no upper limit in ministerial stipends in the Baptist Communion. Each local congregation, being independent, can remunerate its minister above the minimum as it will. It is inevitable that wide disparity should exist.

With the Presbyterian Church of England the situation is different in at least one important particular. While wide disparity in ministerial stipends exists here

---

[1] *Council Report* of the *Congregational Union of England and Wales* of *May 1949* revised these figures again: List A, minimum £290 p.a. and manse. List B, £240 p.a. and manse: town and country to rank alike.

[2] *The New Home Work Fund, 1946*, p. 3; cf. *Report of the Council adopted by the Assembly of the Baptist Union*, p. 11. By 1949 this had been advanced to £282 p.a. and manse.

also, a serious effort is made to see that congregations which pay the largest stipend to their own minister pay a proportionately large contribution to the fund which maintains the minimum stipend for other ministers. Until 1946 this sum was calculated at a definite rate on the minister's stipend alone, and, the higher it rose, the more steeply the outgoing contribution rose also. A congregation could pay £1,000 a year to its minister, but to do that it had to make a heavy contribution to the Sustentation Fund also. The more they paid locally, the more to the central fund.

From 1947 the calculation has been differently based. The contribution of the local church is fixed not in proportion to the minister's stipend but at a percentage, increasing according to a prescribed scale, of the total amount of the contributions of the congregation to *all* Church funds.

The minimum stipend is £300 per annum with a manse (or manse allowance). The rates on the manse are not normally paid by the church but, where they are, the amount is considered as an addition to the minister's stipend. The manse is not provided with furniture by the church, but the house is maintained in repair.

What, then, is the contribution of Methodism to this perplexing problem?

Notice, first, her method in finding and training her ministers. Methodism is still, I believe, the only large section of the Church in our land which regularly takes a lad from the tail of a plough, or the bench of a factory, or a desk in an office, asking nothing whatever about his financial resources until she has decided whether or not he has the call of God—and then makes him one of her ministers, though he (and his folk) may not be able to contribute a single penny to his training.[1] His prepara-

[1] The Salvation Army prefers not to be described as a 'Church'.

tion may take years at Cambridge or in a college linked with a modern university. It matters not. If he is called of God, Methodism undertakes his entire training. His poverty is not so much as mentioned.

There are, of course, scholarships available in the colleges of other Communions, and one does not forget the 'sponsor' system which has been worked with success elsewhere, but I find that the *normality* of this approach to the money problem in Methodism surprises people of other persuasions, and some, indeed, have said that it is 'marvellous in their eyes'.

Notice, in the second place, that without claiming for a moment to have reached the ideal, it may fairly be suggested that Methodism has made a serious and successful effort through two centuries to realize a principle in ministerial allowances which shall fulfil the dictum 'to each according to his need'. It goes without saying that she has asked from her ministers also that they shall give all they have 'according to their ability'.

No Methodist minister may engage in any trade.[1] He cannot use part of his time in gainful commerce. He is under vows to give all his time to the service of God and the Church. If he uses part of his time in authorship, it is expected (though there is no precise rule upon the point) that his writings will be related to the spread of Christian truth. He is a man set apart to holy things. He receives his modest allowances on the understanding that, being freed from acute financial cares, he can give his whole mind to the Gospel of Christ.

He is not primarily the servant of the local church or circuit but of the whole denomination. In the last resort, the whole denomination under God is his security for his status and his 'stipend'. He cannot be 'without

---

[1] The legal basis of this rule has been blurred since Union. Its sharper precision is being considered by the Committee on Methodist Law and Polity.

pastoral charge', except by rare permission. Local officials might shorten his stay in one place but they cannot affect his status in the Church as a whole. He is never in slavery to wealthy laymen.

The 'unemployed minister' who can, in some circumstances, be a pathetic figure, is unknown in Methodism. When the denomination takes and ordains a minister, she undertakes for him too. Acknowledging that he is called of God, she sets him aside by the imposition of hands and seeks to set him free also from gnawing economic care. He will never have a wide margin: sometimes no margin at all, But he will have *enough!*

He will have, moreover, equality with his brethren. Not—it is true—an equality worked out to a pound, but a rough equality. The great majority of 'allowances' in Methodism lie between £330 and £380 per annum for ordained ministers, the sum varying at its minimum level according to the years a man has been in the work. There are no 'plums'. Ripe scholars, keen administrators, the most diligent pastor, and the ablest preacher will all be found within these limits. A small number of appointments run beyond the upper limit, but they are only a handful in the ministry as a whole, and they do not run far.

No Methodist minister receives less than the fixed minimum. It is not unusual in Christian Communions to fix a certain minimum of ministerial allowances *as an aim*. With all the good will in the world, the aim may not be reached.

In Methodism, when the minimum is fixed, it is paid.

This rough equality in allowances has had its own conspicuous share in knitting the Methodist ministry into a close brotherhood. Private means among these men are unusual. They know each other's circumstances and feel a kindred care.

The principle of giving each 'according to his need' involves, of course, family allowances. A man with six children is in greater need than one with three. Two hundred years after Methodism instituted children's allowances, the State took the idea up. No wonder Eleanor Rathbone remarked to a friend in the House of Commons on the day of her triumph with the Family Allowances Bill: 'The Wesleyans were the pioneers in the practice of making family allowances.'[1] Lean as his circumstances were, the Methodist minister had not to dread the birth of another little child in his home even in the hungry 'forties. His Church reached a hand to him again.

Nor was the Church indifferent to the education of the children. Wesley founded himself in 1748 a school which soon became a school for the sons of the preachers, and neither the expense of the schooling nor the migrant character of the itinerant ministry was allowed to be a barrier to an education in harmony with the best standards of each succeeding age.

The allowances of a Methodist minister are sufficiently modest for any man to be secure against the charge of entering the ministry for money, and the fact that there are no highly paid posts to whet ambition secures him also from tainting his holy calling with ideas of worldly advancement. It would be honest to admit that some differences of opinion occasionally occur concerning the right level of allowances. Some few laymen—ill-paid themselves—think the minister is well-paid. The majority of Methodists do not share that view.

The rise in the cost of living does not reflect itself readily in the sums the ministers receive, but it should be noted that the minimum allowances have now gone up by 44 per cent. If account is taken of the cost of living, the income is not large.

[1] *Methodist Recorder*, 22nd February 1945.

Yet, with the provision and maintenance of a furnished house, and his rates paid, the minister is not unaware that his allowances are more, in some ways, than they seem, and when he adds the educational advantages also he is not likely to forget that he is better off than a large number of the people to whom he ministers.

If he sees his school contemporaries in other walks of life easily surpassing him in their ability to secure the goods of this world, he resists any feeling of envy. He deeply believes that the ministry *ought* to be a life of sacrifice. The very power of his words in preaching derive something from the people's knowledge that he has made sacrifices for this way of life, and when things are especially difficult with money he will recall that the honoured rule of the Methodist preacher at all times is not 'as much as we can get' but 'as little as we can live on'.

And, more than all else, this tonic thought braces him: that he is privileged to illustrate to all who heed that the principle toward which the world is groping is workable; that it is possible for men of Christian conviction happily and effectively to live by the rule: 'From each according to his ability: to each according to his need.'

CHAPTER EIGHT

IN ENLISTING THE SERVICE OF LAYMEN.

IT IS FREQUENTLY said that the Church is out of touch with the world. What the people mean who use that phrase is that the *ministry* is out of touch with the world. Even that statement could be sharply disputed. It isn't obvious why ministers who are in touch with people all the days of their lives are any more out of touch with the world than doctors, for instance, or lawyers, or any other body of professional men. The confessions they hear, the private problems they share, and the guidance they are called upon to give, develop a knowledge of the human heart which is quite unusual. One can be in touch with life without working in a factory or idling in a club.

But even if it were true that the ministry is out of touch with the world, it would still not prove that the *Church* is out of touch with the world.

When were the ministry and the Church equated? What heretical abandonment of the grand doctrine of the 'priesthood of all believers' could lead to such confusion? Are not the laity as much a part of the Church as those who administer the sacraments? Can any robust Protestant tacitly consent to a true distinction between the professionally 'religious' and the rest?

Where Christ is, there is the Church, and the Church is in touch with the world wherever a devout navvy—his heart full of Christ—digs up the road with his gang; wherever the Christian ploughman drives a straight furrow and sits down to his meal with his mates; wherever the Christian clerk, or smith, or sailor, lives in the power of his Lord and bears his witness before his fellows.

If anyone wanted to prove the impotence of the Church and its slight effect upon social life, he should not concentrate on the unworldliness of parsons and their supposed detachment from affairs but rather on the dumbness of the Christian laity and their unwillingness to speak of the Lord they genuinely love. The parson's condemnation is that he fails so often to make the layman vocal. In an age when only a small part of the community comes to the preaching of the Christian Gospel, the supreme opportunity of imparting the message belongs to those who, in their normal business relations, make contact every day with the unbelieving multitude and can impress them with the way of Christ.

It is one thing to contend with heat for the priesthood of all believers: it is another thing to fulfil those priestly functions conscientiously, understandingly, and with religious zeal.

The first function of a priest which comes to the mind of most people is that of intercession. The priest goes to God for the people. He is the accepted intermediary of earth and heaven. That was true, of course, of the Hebrew priests, and the priests of paganism. It belongs to the office as such. No priest goes to God for himself alone. Anybody can do that. The distinctive character of the priest is this: he intercedes for others. He goes in a representative capacity: not *only* for himself—not *chiefly* for himself: he goes in ambassadorial status for his fellows. Let any layman, sensitive to the danger of ministerial arrogance (resenting, perhaps, the very word 'layman' with its flavour of inferiority), and holding with firmness to the priesthood of all believers, test himself here: 'How much do I intercede for others? Do I go often to God for the people who do not go for themselves? Is the strength and the power and the passion of my prayers that these others may believe?'

Anyone who believes in God—and some, even, who say they don't—will pray earnestly for himself and his dearest in personal distress. In anxiety, the prayerless man will plead for his sick wife or child. Many women, normally neglectful of God, stormed heaven for their boys when they were in peril at the war. It is all natural and understandable . . . but it is not priestly. God does not spurn the prayer, but neither can He miss the selfishness in it.

Here is the uniqueness of the priest. He will intercede

with passion and persistence for those who are *not* his own. It does not require the spur of self-interest to drive him to his knees. He has what our fathers called 'the burden of souls' and he yearns for people with whom he is linked by no tie of blood and—on their side—no bond of affection at all. He takes the world's sorrows on himself and in the name of the world's Redeemer he bears those sins and woes and follies to the Father-God above.

It is idle to boast about the priesthood of all believers if we are neglectful of the solemn duties that priesthood implies. It is vain to protest one's disbelief in any other priestly 'orders' and our essential equality in Christ if we fail in this first of functions—secret, incessant, intercessory prayer.

But not only does a priest intercede with God for the people: he intercedes also with the people for God. The priestly function has this two-fold aspect. The priest goes to God for the people. He goes also to the people for God.

Let us be frank and admit that this involves tasks from which, by nature and social convention, we shrink. In England it is regarded as improper to talk about religion on non-religious occasions. It isn't done.

When Samuel Rogers was asked his religion, he said that it was the religion of all sensible men. He countered the next question (an inquiry what that might be) by saying that all sensible men kept it to themselves.

One remembers the man stopped in the street and asked by a religious zealot: 'Have you met God?'

'I'll tell you whom I have met,' he answered. 'I've met a very impertinent man.'

Englishmen hate to have their souls burgled. The mass of our fellow-countrymen most strongly resent being jockeyed into a corner and asked if they're 'saved'.

Even if we brushed the question of courtesy aside on the

principle that no one need be too concerned about courtesy in getting a man off a sinking ship, it is still bad tactics to antagonize anybody one wants to win.

Yet—having said that—the priestly obligation still remains. Somehow or other, with all the skill and craft we can command, we must rise to our responsibilities and intercede with the people for God.

Nor must it be supposed that that only implies public preaching. It is one of the major errors of the modern Church to suppose that her evangelism belongs only to her public preachers, and it is a still more grievous mistake to suppose that it belongs only to the ministry. Such a belief was not held in the Early Church and it has never been accepted in times of evangelical vigour. It is the responsibility of the whole Church, and—as we have seen—in this age it falls with especial weight upon the laity. Theirs is the contact. Every day they are in touch with those who do not believe. With sincere affection, with skill, with sensitivity, and with constraining power, they must present the paramount claims of Christ.

The steward of a Methodist church told me once—and told me with delight—that he had been doing business with a man for twenty years and they had just made an astonishing discovery. They had both been, during the whole of that period, officials of their respective churches but neither knew that the other was in this way of life at all.

Really?!

One would have thought that some quality in their lives, some distinctiveness in business dealing, some difference of manner or emphasis would have broken through the crust of commerce and revealed the prime allegiance of their souls.

Is it so easy to conceal the love of our Lord? Is a Christian, even in business, so similar to everybody else that it is impossible to guess who he is?

I knew a young, unmarried man who fell out of work during the long trade depression between the wars. He was a skilled workman and a fine Christian, but how he lived during those lean years I hardly know. His joy when, at last, he got a job in a wireless factory, it would be difficult to describe.

There was, however, a fly in the ointment. He soon found out that the men with whom he was working regularly used the most filthy language and it was impossible to close his ears all the time to their obscenities.

He was a gentle soul . . . and yet bold with the boldness of those who belong to our 'royal priesthood'. He could not feel that it was right to make no protest. To toss on a sea of blasphemy and hear the high and holy name of God profaned every ten minutes was more than he could stand. At the beginning of his second week he told a few of them gently, affectionately, but plainly, how he felt. A word, he hoped, would be enough.

It was a vain hope. They laughed till they cried and blasphemed the more.

So he got a box—a collecting-box from the local infirmary—and put in a penny whenever they swore. He knew it was odd, but he was a simple soul and wondered how to make them realize how much their obscenities scorched his soul.

When they first realized what he was doing, they swore the harder. They encouraged one another in it. They said that it was their first opportunity to curse for the cure of the sick. After being out of work for years, that poor, brave, obscure disciple put, by his own act, nearly all his first week's wages in the box.

But he broke them. When they saw what he had done, something happened. The Spirit of God used the simple artifice of it. The sacrifice sobered and shamed them. In its own little way, it was like a glimpse of the Cross.

They saw how much it hurt him and the blasphemy and obscenity died down. Indeed, it became rare. In the passing of time, when it happened, it happened only by accident, and it was followed immediately by an apology and the offender himself paid the 'fine'.

He was a plain, working man, speaking with a provincial accent, but he belonged to the royal priesthood. He put the Church in touch with the world. It could be said of him, as it was said of Manning: '*Sacerdos* was written right across his brow.'

I judge a priest not by the vestments he wears. The test is two-fold. Does he plead in secret with God for the people? Does he witness before the people to the things of God? That working man did both. He burgled no one's soul, but, on the other hand, he was not dumb concerning his Lord. He did not match his mates' blasphemous speech with blasphemous silence. He cared. He cared for their souls more than he cared for convention, or peace, or his own money. He led not a few to faith.

How can we open the mouths of the laity? Prebendary Wilson Carlile said in a well-known phrase: 'I have got the biggest job I have ever tackled in my life. I am trying to open the mouths of the people in the pews.' Dr. J. H. Oldham believes that the future of civilization lies largely in the hands of the laity. Dr. Emil Brunner has asserted that 'the time of the *Pfarrerkirche* is definitely past', by which he means that the age of '*the Minister Church*' is over: the church in which one man carries the real responsibility, with the congregation not so much in partnership as in varying degrees of acquiescence.[1]

It is not seriously disputed by those who know the facts that Methodism has had unusual skill in opening the mouths of the laity and in placing spiritual responsibility squarely on their shoulders.

[1] *The Divine Imperative*, p. 558.

At first glance this may not appear to be true. No layman can come to the prime place in the Methodist Church as President of the Conference in the way a layman can preside over the meetings of the Baptist or Congregational Union. Nor are these presiding offices parallel whosoever occupies them, for the Methodist Conference is a legislative body which regulates the life of all the churches of the Communion, while the Baptist and Congregational Unions are meetings composed of representatives of local congregations which forfeit none of their independency to the Annual Assembly at which they choose to confer.

Only in exceptional circumstances can a layman administer the sacrament in Methodism, and ministers preside at all business meetings.

Yet it remains true that Methodism has had unusual success in opening the mouths of the laity and in placing high spiritual responsibility upon them.

It is estimated that five out of every seven Methodist services conducted in England are conducted by laymen. There are 25,817 fully accredited local preachers in British Methodism alone, and 3,175 on trial. None of our sister Churches makes anything approaching this use of the lay preacher. It is the simple, unexaggerated truth to say that the Methodist Church could not function for a week without this volume of consecrated help.

Drawn from every walk of life: lords, cabinet ministers, rank-and-file Members of Parliament, from all the professions and most segments of business life—tinker, tailor, soldier, sailor—they make 'an exceeding great army', and what their work and witness have meant to the life of England is beyond human computation.

It amuses some people to disparage the work of the local preacher. It is suggested that, in every department of life, the age of the 'amateur' is over: that the general level of education is such that people demand to be served by a 'professional' and that the most a local preacher can ever be is a substitute. Even when—as often happens—the local preacher is a highly cultured man and, indeed, an expert in his own walk of life, he is still, it is said, an amateur in the pulpit, and the appreciation he receives is partly compounded of the kind recognition that 'after all, it isn't his job'.

I contest all that. Without depreciating for a moment the importance of specialized research, or supposing that any but very rare men can be deep theologians by spare-time study alone, I contend that in a religion which is at heart a way of life, experience of that way of life in the work-a-day world is great equipment for preaching it.

Most ministers are aware that if there are gains in their professional status and training (and, of course, there are) there are losses too. Who that has carried the Gospel to the people outside—to folk in a factory or works' canteen —but knows that look (slightly amused and slightly cynical) with which they regard the parson and which says as plainly as any words: 'That's right, mate. Do your stuff. You're *paid* to say that'?

They cannot look like that at a layman. They might still think him a fool, but his motives puzzle them and they find it hard to resist the conviction that he believes his message himself.

I know no way of circumventing this cynicism in a *short* time but by the witness of consecrated laymen. The layman is the ordinary infantryman of the advancing host of God. He must engage the enemy at close hand. He stands in the fighting line every day and deserves the honour that belongs to those who come to grips with the foe. The greatest service the minister can render to the people outside is to make the consecrated laity as informed in the faith and as incisive in witness as he possibly can.

And when the layman steps into the pulpit as a local preacher he still retains the advantages of his non-professional status. Let his humility bear witness that he is not there because 'he likes to hear himself speak' and the people will not forget that he is not there either for any pecuniary advantage, but that all his thought and his study and his testimony are an offering to the glory of God.

The influence of such men in a village community is immense. It is hardly less influential in a town.

Some of the greatest preachers of all time have belonged to this order.

Dr. J. H. Shakespeare has spoken of the prophetic preaching he has heard from these men in Norfolk and in Cornwall.[1] Dr. R. F. Horton, with more than a little of the fastidiousness of an Oxford Don, put a local preacher first of all the men he ever heard proclaim the Gospel of the Living Lord. He was a carpenter in the Isle of Man.

Our first Sunday the services were taken by the most plain and unpretentious man that I had ever seen in a pulpit. His face was marked with lines of thought and care. His voice was untunable, and his diction merely that of the street. But we were at once brought into an atmosphere of reality. In the morning he spoke on knowing God, and tears of deep feeling welled in our eyes as he showed how he had come to know God, not from books, but in the workshop; not by arguments, but by the stern discipline of a workman's life. We were eager to go again in the evening; he spoke on the words, 'to live is Christ'. It was all drawn from experience. He taught me a twofold lesson, that effective preaching must have practical points of contact with the lives of the hearers, and must be wrought out in the life of the preacher. Through fulfilling these conditions these

[1] *The Churches at the Cross-Roads*, p. 54.

two addresses, badly delivered, and without pretence of form or construction, were better than any sermons I had been able to preach. I knew that in God's sight they were on a higher level.

During my Oxford days I heard most of the great Anglican preachers: Liddon, Lightfoot, Bishop Magee, Bishop Alexander; and since then I have listened to most of the preachers held in repute among Free Churchmen. But I cannot say that any of them affected me as that carpenter did.[1]

While local preachers were never appointed lightly, today their admission in all but the most extraordinary cases requires that they pass a serious written examination in Bible Knowledge and Christian Doctrine. To maintain and renew the ranks of her local preachers is one of Methodism's most solemn obligations to herself and to the whole cause of religion in our land. Her local preachers constantly supply the pulpits of other Free Churches too.

But the contribution of Methodism to English Christendom in opening the mouths of the laity is not confined to the local preachers. Wesley had not a great deal to say himself about local preachers, and most of what he did say was critical.[2] The term was used somewhat differently in the eighteenth century. While it over-simplifies the historical record a little, it is roughly true to say that many who began as 'local preachers' became 'travelling preachers' (later called ministers), while the precursors of those we now describe as local preachers were 'exhorters'.

But Wesley made the widest use of the consecrated laity as class-leaders. These men and women were incomparably more influential in early Methodism than those we now call local preachers. Many of them were

---

[1] *Autobiography*, pp. 150f.
[2] e.g. *Journal*, Vol. VII, p. 128; *Letters*, Vols. IV, p. 161; VII, pp. 88, 94.

outstanding evangelists—though they seldom or never preached. They worked individually, inviting people to the class-meeting and dealing personally with them until they found God and were seeking 'perfect love'.

These leaders were made the under-pastors of the flock: almost the pastors themselves. They were hand-picked men and women with a deep experience of God and they were given responsibility for the spiritual growth of a dozen of their fellows. The women were barely less prominent than the men. Their little flock was often composed of 'finders' and 'seekers' as well. They met weekly and spoke of their experience of God. It was the leader's business to 'open their mouths'. He told of how God had dealt with him and encouraged them to witness as well. To remain dumb in such company was almost unknown and even regarded as dishonouring to God. Having tasted His favour, who could be silent about it? Even if the great experience had not come, the seeker could vent his yearnings, and the others would inflame his desires with the assurance that the experience was only a little ahead.

So they built each other up! So they fanned the flame of devotion in each other's heart! So these little cells of vital spiritual life brought health again to the social body in a thousand hamlets and villages, and even in the cities they had their modest part in saving society from corruption.

The structure of Methodism in this regard remains essentially the same after two hundred years. We are painfully aware that the class-meeting is not as common or as healthy as it was and that the number of our local preachers declines.

But nothing can alter the primacy and key position of lay service in Methodism which does not alter the very character of Methodism itself.

If it astonishes a militant Free Churchman that a minister should preside at every business meeting in Methodism, and he is tempted to suppose that this is a clerical-ridden Church, let him take heed that it is in the *preaching* and the *teaching* of this Church that the laity have so large a share. Methodism does not accept the easy distinction between the temporal and spiritual affairs of the Church, handing one over to the laity and retaining the other for the ministry. Stephen was chosen *to serve tables* because he was full of the Holy Ghost.

Moreover, there is no way to keep the laity dumb so effectively as to confine them to the material concerns of the Church. If we want the ordinary members to be incapable of giving a reason for the faith that is in them and too shy to say in normal common-sense English a good word for Jesus Christ, let us give them no more to do than keeping the accounts, and looking after the heating apparatus, and giving out the hymn-books.

But if we want them to be both spiritually mature and guidedly vocal, let us share the preaching and the teaching with them; and be students together of the Word and colleagues in evangelism, and we shall move England again as once our fathers did.

Some people among us have been looking wistfully at denominations which almost always provide one minister for one church, and it is not uncommon for keen young ministers to sigh for more concentration in preaching.

But it is folly to toy with the idea of 'one-minister one-church' in Methodism. It could be done only by ruthlessly cutting down the number of our churches or immensely enlarging the ministry. Does anyone seriously desire that a single church be closed which isn't plainly redundant, or the evangelical Gospel silenced in a thousand villages? Does anyone suppose that we have either the men or the money to quadruple the ministry?

And if we had both the men and the money, it is open to question if it would be a good thing to do. It is closer to our genius and nearer to the nation's need to give ourselves anew to the task in which we have had unusual success: the maintenance and enlarging of that order of laymen who have ever been among the glories of our Church and who, as class-leaders and local preachers, have been such true pastors of the flock. If, as Hugh Price Hughes believed, the ministers hold Methodism in the palm of their hand, it is largely for this: that, like their Lord, they should concentrate much of their time on the training of a few—a few to whom, as time passes, the many will owe so much.

The ministry is spread out far more thinly on the Mission Field than in rural England, but the Word wins its widening way. Prebendary Wilson Carlile, and Dr. J. H. Oldham, and Dr. Emil Brunner, all of whom viewed the need of the world and of the Church from outside Methodism, unite with a hundred other discerning minds in affirming that our present urgent need is an evangelizing laity: those who—being instructed in the faith—might serve in pulpit or on platform but would most certainly witness in the world.

Any Communion which can raise them, and teach her sister Churches how to raise them too, will render a service to the whole of Christendom.

Let Methodism still show the way!

EPILOGUE

WE LIVE in grey times. The darkness which followed the blinding flash of the atomic bomb when it burst above Hiroshima on 6th August 1945 has crept like an impalpable shadow across the world and we move about in the after-gloom. Truly our future is all unknown and the hearts of men fail because of fear.

It is not surprising, therefore, that many Christians, not normally or deeply interested in apocalyptics, should catch themselves wondering whether some catastrophic consummation is at hand and listen with something more than amused contempt to the people who specialize in discerning 'the signs of the times' and assert that the end of all things is at hand.

In some ways, it doesn't matter if it is.

> *Sleep after toil, port after stormy seas,*
> *Ease after war, death after life, does greatly please.*

When the worse comes to the worst for the Christian, the good has but become the best.

Heaven!!

Is that a doom to dread?

It would be mistaken, however, to suppose that the mass of Christian thought has turned that way. Most Christians are still of opinion that God does not even yet despair of our race and that the prayer which Jesus taught us to pray—'Thy will be done in earth as it is in heaven'—will have a glorious fulfilment. The knowledge of the Lord, it is confidently predicted, will cover the earth as the waters cover the sea. Good will eventually triumph. 'We shall see', these thinkers say, 'not only the goodness of the Lord but the victory of that goodness in the land of the living.'

It is fortunate that this variation of view makes no difference to the Christian's plain duty from day to day. The clamant task is evangelism either way. Howsoever we view cosmic events, this urgent undeniable duty demands to be done. It should not be one whit more

imperative for those who are preparing to sing *Dies irae*
than for those who see the slow unfolding of future
centuries and the gradual triumph in things terrestrial of
the statesmanship of God.

Using whatsoever gifts we have, and not equating the
word 'evangelism' with one particular method of
bringing men to Christ, we must all bend our strength to
the supreme task we have been given to do.

'Go ye therefore and make disciples of all the nations....'
That is our commission! The passing years only confirm
its primacy. We have seen Our Lord permanently change
individuals; we have seen Him transform families and
factories; we believe He could do no less for cities and
communities; we hold that He could save the world.

He sweeps His sceptre over every area of life. Disciple-
ship begins in the surrender of the will and in personal
devotion, but it cannot end there. We must carry it to
every phase of human activity: to art and commerce,
labour and leisure, sport and science, legislation and
education. All are His.

In the privilege of evangelism, none is exempt from
responsibility. Men and women; laymen and ministers;
the young, the middle-aged, and the old people; the
toilers with hand and brain—scholar, statesman, engineer;
—evangelism, in its widest meaning, requires them all.

Nor is the urgency of the task to be found only in the
world's condition. It is to be found also in our human
awareness of the passage of time. We may find it hard to
say *what* has passed when time has passed, but it isn't hard
to point to changes in ourselves.

The comb passes through the hair more swiftly. Something of resilience has gone. Whatever else may not have
passed, a great many opportunities have passed for ever.
We dare not fritter any more away. The night cometh

when no man can work. A double urgency, therefore, hangs over the enterprise. The world's condition cries aloud for the eternal Gospel, and the galloping years carry away our chances of serving it.

Nor does the wisest among us know what opportunities are left nor how soon upon our day of life the night will fall.

A friend of mine told me once that he had reduced a normal life to the length of one day in order to test how far he was forward on the pilgrimage of life. He assumed that life was seventy years and that a normal day runs from seven o'clock in the morning till eleven o'clock at night.

That being so, he worked it out *roughly* like this: At 20 years of age it is half-past eleven; at 30, it is two o'clock; at 40, it is four o'clock; at 50, half-past six; at 60, a quarter to nine.

What time is it with you?

Whatever the time o' day, let us do all we can. Howsoever our energies may flag, let nothing challenge our initial consecration or blur the vision of our evangelical task. In the difficult middle years, wilting beneath the destruction that wasteth at noonday, let us still go on with a fine scorn of earthly fame and fortune, and let it be our high resolve never to be traitorous in heart.

Our natural sphere of service will be in that branch of the Church in which it has pleased God to save our soul. To know with intimacy our spiritual heritage; to count it a privilege to serve people who, for the most part, are poor and unpretentious; to follow a way of life largely devoid of social distinction and yet to know by every means of knowledge open to humankind that this is the work of God and His will for us—there is the joy as there also is our duty, and in that double motivation let us labour till the day is done.

And if, at the end of the day, a little time is allowed to

sit over the fire and think, though we know ourselves to be unprofitable servants and base no hopes of the future on our own endeavours, it will not be without comfort to remember that we laboured while it was day: that the way home is plain and that we may yet catch the thrilling accents of the Master: 'Well done, good and faithful servant, enter into the joy of thy Lord.'

QUESTIONS FOR DISCUSSION

CHAPTER ONE

1. Is it true of religious institutions, as of individuals, that those who lose their lives shall save them? What about our Lord's phrase 'for my sake'?
2. At what point could the legitimate love of a man's denomination lead him into error?
3. In what order would you put the unfinished tasks of Methodism if their urgency was the first thought in your mind?
4. This sevenfold division of the distinctive work of Methodism does not exhaust her unfulfilled mission. What other concerns would you include?

CHAPTER TWO

1. Why is the doctrine of Christian Perfection neglected in Methodism today?
2. Analyse in thought and then describe to others the person you know (or knew) who most reminded you of Jesus Christ.
3. What does it mean to live a 'moment-by-moment' life? Relate this to John 17 [3].
4. Pose this question to yourself: 'How good could God make me?'

CHAPTER THREE

1. A man said: 'I suppose we are all more or less and to some extent "born again".' What is foolish in this statement? But how did he come to make it? Are there any instances of 'gradual conversion' in the New Testament? Can a thing come both gradually and at a moment?
2. Some people believe that prayers read from a book can't be 'from the heart'. What do they mean? How do we learn to pray 'from the heart'?
3. Draw up a free form of worship, choosing hymns, lessons, and sermon-theme, making it a unity and (for

a reverent congregation) a *complete* act of worship. Is such a form 'free' from the congregation's point of view?

4. What do you mean by a 'good' sermon? Are people wrong who go to church hoping for one? Ought a worshipper to 'enjoy' a service?

CHAPTER FOUR

1. If a man is truly devout, does it matter what his politics are?
2. What has given currency to the phrase that religion is 'the opium of the people'?
3. Is it a bad thing that a denomination draws its members mainly from one class—or might it be an anticipation of a class-less society?
4. Is it an adequate solution of the problems relating capital to labour to say that we just need 'the team-spirit in industry'? What ought Christians to mean by 'the team-spirit'?

CHAPTER FIVE

1. Would Church Reunion mean that all Christians would have to worship in the same way and think precisely the same about *everything*?
2. 'The reason why theological controversy has abated is not chiefly that modern Christians have more love for one another but because they hold the truth less firmly than their fathers did.' Do you agree? When, if ever, is this kind of 'controversy' a good thing?
3. Examine the belief that a divided Church cannot be an evangelizing Church. If it applies to the local church, does it also apply to the whole of Christ's Church militant here on earth?
4. What can you do *now*, and in your own neighbourhood, to heal the divisions of Christendom?

CHAPTER SIX

1. In your experience does the chillness between 'church' and 'chapel', which survives in some rural areas, have more to do with social and spiritual snobberies than

with any serious difference about religion? If there are faults here, are they all on one side?

2. Imagine for a moment all the Free Church chapels wiped out from the hamlets and villages of England. Attempt to estimate the loss to the whole land. Would there be a similar loss if all the Anglican churches were wiped out?

3. 'People in the country live a less distracted and often a more thoughtful life than those in towns.' Is this true?—and, if so, what advantage can a preacher derive from it? Does it mean that he should have two kinds of sermon?

4. If a town circuit 'adopted' a country circuit, suggest what each might give the other. If a country circuit 'adopted' a slum mission, what then?

CHAPTER SEVEN

1. Is a man who resents the fact that others receive more money for less and lighter work than he himself receives (*a*) jealous, or (*b*) seeking justice, or (*c*) serving the Kingdom of God?

2. When a man is paid wages, what is he paid *for?* A Cabinet Minister is paid £100 a week, and a cabinet maker £6. 6. 0. Can the difference be justified?

3. Do you believe in 'the great minister', i.e. a man of God exalted above his fellows in rank, residence, and remuneration? Does the Church as an institution require its leaders clothed that way? Describe the alternative.

4. Can you even *foresee* the time when men will work for the glory of God and—their needs being met—ask no other reward? Can you mention any such people either (*a*) in Christian history, or (*b*) in the life of today?

CHAPTER EIGHT

1. Is the word 'layman' a word of inferiority? In its ecclesiastical sense, *ought* it to be?

2. A man said: 'My mother was a saint. There were many signs of it but one of them was this: she never looked at the circuit plan to see who was preaching.' What did he mean?

3. How can a man know when it is the will of God that he speak to another man about the claims of Christ? Are there rules—or must he cultivate some inner intuition? What should he do if in doubt?

4. Make a list of the advantages a layman enjoys as against a minister in the work of evangelism. How can *you* be an evangelist? Reduce the answer to 'brass-tacks '.

INDEX OF NAMES

PURNELL AND SONS LTD. PAULTON (SOMERSET) AND LONDON